WE
BAPTISTS

CONTRIBUTORS

The following members of the BWA Study Commissions (1995–1999) have contributed to this book by writing, revising, evaluating, and/or correcting its contents.

Gary L. Abbott
Eljee Bentley
Gerald L. Borchert
C. W. Brister
L. Russ Bush III
L. A. (Tony) Cupit
William R. Estep Jr.
Paul S. Fiddes
James Leo Garrett Jr. (editor-in-chief)
Stanley J. Grenz

David P. Gushee
Brian Haymes
James B. (Jim) Henry
Thorwald Lorenzen
Ken R. Manley
Emmanuel L. McCall Sr.
Doran C. McCarty
Bruce Milne
Richard V. Pierard
James E. Wood Jr.

SPONSORING CHURCHES

The following congregations have generously made monetary contributions so as to make possible the publication of this book:

Broadway Baptist Church, Fort Worth, Texas
Christian Fellowship Baptist Church, College Park, Georgia
Columbus Avenue Baptist Church, Waco, Texas, in memory of
    Mrs. Adrian (Margaret) Vaughan
First Baptist Church, Arlington, Texas
First Baptist Church, Huntsville, Alabama
First Baptist Church, Macon, Georgia
First Baptist Church, Milledgeville, Georgia
First Baptist Church, Orlando, Florida
First Baptist Church, Shreveport, Louisiana
First Baptist Church, Vancouver, British Columbia, Canada
First Baptist Church, Yazoo City, Mississippi, in memory of Owen Cooper
    and in honor of Mrs. Owen (Elizabeth) Cooper
University Baptist Church, Fort Worth, Texas

WE BAPTISTS

Study and Research Division
Baptist World Alliance

PROVIDENCE HOUSE PUBLISHERS
Franklin, Tennessee

Copyright 1999 by Study and Research Division, Baptist World Alliance

All rights reserved. Written permission must be secured from the publisher to use or reproduce any part of this book, except for brief quotations in critical reviews or articles.

Scripture quotations used in this book are from four sources: Revised Standard Version of the Bible. Copyright © 1946, 1952 Division of Christian Education of the National Council of the Churches of Christ in the United States of America. The New English Bible. Copyright © 1961, 1970 Oxford University Press. The Jerusalem Bible. Copyright © 1966 Darton, Longman and Todd, Ltd., and Doubleday and Company, Inc. The Holy Bible, New International Version. Copyright © 1973, 1978, 1984 International Bible Society.

Printed in the United States of America

03   02   01   00   99   1   2   3   4   5

Library of Congress Catalog Card Number: 99-70372

ISBN: 1-57736-143-1

James Leo Garrett Jr., Editor-in-Chief

Cover design by Gary Bozeman

PROVIDENCE HOUSE PUBLISHERS
238 Seaboard Lane • Franklin, Tennessee 37067
800-321-5692
www.providencehouse.com

Contents

Abbreviations	vi
Preface	vii
1. Baptists: A Global Community of Faith	1
2. What Baptists Believe	19
3. How Baptists Make Moral Decisions	34
4. Baptists in Worship	48
5. Baptist Church Life and Leadership	62
6. Human Rights for All	76
Suggestions for Further Reading	87

Abbreviations

ABC	American Baptist Convention; American Baptist Churches U.S.A.
ABCFM	American Board of Commissioners for Foreign Missions
ABFMS	American Baptist Foreign Mission Society
ABHMS	American Baptist Home Mission Society
ABMU	American Baptist Missionary Union
ABPS	American Baptist Publication and Sunday School Society
BMS	Baptist Missionary Society
BWA	Baptist World Alliance
FMB	Foreign Mission Board
JB	Jersualem Bible
NBC	Northern Baptist Convention
NEB	New English Bible
NIV	New International Version
RSV	Revised Standard Version
SBC	Southern Baptist Convention
SBC-FMB	Southern Baptist Convention–Foreign Mission Board

Preface

Who are the Baptists? Are they a cult, a sect, or a Christian denomination? What was their origin, how did they spread, and where may they be found today? How do they perceive the Great Commission of Jesus?

What do Baptists believe, together with other Christians, about God's nature and self-disclosure, the creation of all things, humanity and sin, the saving work of Jesus Christ, becoming and being a Christian, and the last things? What do they affirm as Baptists about Christ as Lord, the authority of the Bible, the work of the Holy Spirit, the church as congregation, believer's baptism by immersion, the priesthood of all believers, the ordained ministry, the Lord's Supper, and religious freedom?

How do Baptists make ethical decisions today? What of grace and works, freedom and responsibility, Jesus as Lord in the congregation, the Bible and its interpretation, and secular wisdom?

Why do Baptists worship the triune God if not because God is worthy of such worship? What different models of worship may be found among Baptists? Why corporate worship and both order and freedom? What are the roles of the Bible, music, the ordinances, giving, and prayer? What results should flow from worship?

How do Baptists conduct their life together in congregations? Why do Baptists insist upon conversion or personal faith prior to church membership? What is meant by mission and servanthood and by the gifts of the Holy Spirit? How do ordained ministers share ministry with all members in a Baptist church? How likely are suffering and sacrifice for church leaders?

We Baptists

What has been the historic passion of Baptists for freedom? What have Baptists stood for in respect to religious freedom vis-à-vis civil government? What is today's worldwide situation concerning the denial or abuse of basic human rights? How does knowledge lead to responsibility? How have Baptists expanded their concern for religious freedom to include the advocacy of human rights, and what are they doing today about human rights?

The six study commissions of the Baptist World Alliance for the quinquennium 1995–1999 have attempted to provide answers to these questions both for Baptist readers who wish to know more about the Baptist movement in which they are participants and for non-Baptist readers who desire to have more accurate information and insights about the Baptists.

The six chapters of this book, although reflective of the work of the study commissions that comprise the Study and Research Division of the Baptist World Alliance, by no means reflect the entire ministry and mission of the Baptist World Alliance. Its Evangelism and Education Division and its World Aid, Communications, and Development committees have their distinctive tasks. Readers of *We Baptists*, for example, can profit from L. A. (Tony) Cupit's *Biblical Models for Evangelism: 1st Century Strategies for the 21st Century* (McLean, VA: Baptist World Alliance, 1997).

You are encouraged to read *We Baptists* and then gather a group of fellow believers to read and discuss it.

CHAPTER ONE

Baptists:
A Global Community of Faith

BAPTISTS HAVE GROWN FROM A TINY HANDFUL OF PERSECUTED believers to a global community which today is one of the largest Protestant groupings in the world. This chapter will attempt to show how that happened. Such growth should help Baptists to function more effectively in the twenty-first century.

THE BIRTH OF THE BAPTIST MOVEMENT

Baptists can trace their antecedents to the Protestant Reformation of the sixteenth century. One group of reformers, the Anabaptists, some of whom are called Mennonites, taught many of the principles Baptists came to call their own. They insisted that a true church includes only those who have repented of their sins and have been baptized as born-again believers in Jesus Christ. They affirmed that Christ alone is Lord of the church, the Bible is the final source of authority, and discipleship is the core of the Great Commission. In spiritual matters churches are subject only to Christ. God ordained the state to care for the physical well-being of society but gave it no power to function as a spiritual guardian. It may not authorize or establish a specific form of worship or prohibit any religion it does not like.

As an organized movement, Baptists originated in England, after a brief sojourn in Holland, at the beginning of the seventeenth century.

We Baptists

Many people there felt that the Church of England, which had been refashioned during the Reformation, had not gone far enough in removing Roman Catholic practices and developing genuinely evangelical doctrine. It was ruled by bishops and established as the official church with the king or queen as its supreme governor on earth. The main body of dissenters, the Puritans, remained within the Anglican Church (another name for the Church of England) and worked for further reform.

Others, called Separatists, left the church because they saw no hope for real change. Since the English monarch persecuted all those who did not worship as the church prescribed, some Separatists left the country and sought refuge in Holland, the only place in Europe where religious toleration existed. One group of Separatists, from the area of Gainsborough, led by John Smyth, a former teacher at the University of Cambridge, arrived in Amsterdam (Holland) in 1608.

Faced with a variety of religious options in their new home, Smyth's followers felt compelled to examine the Bible carefully. They concluded that infant baptism was contrary to the New Testament. Obedient discipleship required that the church be formed on the basis of personal profession of faith followed by baptism. The acceptance of believer's baptism further separated them from their fellow Separatists as well as from Anglicans and Puritans. Smyth wrote a confession of faith in 1612 in which he affirmed that "Christ only is the king and lawgiver of the church and conscience," thus advocating for the first time in English both religious liberty and separation of church and state.

Thomas Helwys, a gentleman farmer who had gone to Holland with Smyth, returned home in 1612 and established the first Baptist church on English soil at Spitalfields, just outside London. Soon thereafter, he published a book, *A Short Declaration of the Mistery of Iniquity*. It built on Smyth's statement and declared that the king had no jurisdiction in matters of religion, for one's religion was a matter solely between the individual and God. This principle of freedom applied to all—Roman Catholics, Jews, Muslims, and even pagans. Helwys's teaching became a foundation stone of Baptist beliefs. His boldness was costly, for he was sent to Newgate Prison, where he died as the first Baptist martyr. Smyth died in exile in Amsterdam (1612).

Before long, a variety of Baptist churches had sunk roots into English soil. Those similar to the Spitalfields church were called General Baptists and accepted the Arminian view that Christ had died for all people. The Particular Baptists leaned toward the Calvinist posi-

Baptists: A Global Community of Faith

tion that he had died only for those whom God had predestined or elected to save. In 1644, seven Particular Baptist congregations issued the First London Confession of Faith. This was a moderately Calvinistic statement that softened the emphasis on predestination, focusing on the salvation available in Christ. It affirmed immersion as the proper form of believer's baptism. A revision made two years later enlarged the articles on religious freedom in the manner of Smyth and Helwys. The London and other early Baptist confessions also upheld the doctrine of God as Trinity, the need for spiritual rebirth, and the requirement of baptism for membership in a congregation. But they rejected the charge that they were "Anabaptists" (re-baptizers), because they regarded infant baptism as no baptism at all, and referred to themselves as "baptized believers in Christ." Before the end of the century, they were called "Baptists."

Thus, basic Baptist distinctives were firmly in place by the end of the seventeenth century. The church is a community of professing believers who have found new life through repentance and faith in Christ. Believer's baptism is the act of initiation into the visible church, and immersion is the form by which it is to be administered. Individual believers have freedom of conscience. They can study the Scriptures themselves and follow God wherever the Holy Spirit leads them. The state has no authority to exercise influence or control over the church, since Christ alone is its head. At the same time, individual Baptists are free to participate actively in public life and have done so through the centuries.

THE MOVEMENT EXPANDS

Baptist historians often use the illustration that England was the puddle into which the stone fell, and the ripples spread first within Britain, then to America, and eventually throughout the entire world. This movement outward occurred in two ways. First, Baptists evangelized people in their own areas; they, in turn, communicated the gospel message to others. During the 1640s and 1650s, the period of the English Civil War and the rule of Oliver Cromwell, Baptists experienced remarkable growth. Several Anglican clergymen joined their ranks, while Cromwell's army included many Baptists. The godly soldiers carried the message into Scotland, Wales, and Ireland and left congregations behind. During the 1600s, Baptists also crossed the Atlantic and founded churches in the American colonies.

WE BAPTISTS

The other element in Baptist expansion, cross-cultural missionary work, became prominent in the late eighteenth and early nineteenth centuries with the founding of the Baptist Missionary Society (BMS) in 1792 in Britain and the Triennial Convention in the United States in 1814. Yet Baptists' direct evangelism among people of their own country and their foreign missionary work so intersected that it is difficult to separate them for discussion. One thing is clear: the conviction that Christians must evangelize is central to the Baptist faith, and this made religious freedom imperative. Those to whom the gospel is preached must be free to respond as they are moved by the Holy Spirit. They should not be coerced by any human agent, whether it be the state or an established church.

The eighteenth century was a difficult time for English Baptists. Some General Baptists questioned the divinity of Christ and became Unitarians. Reacting to this theological liberalism, many Particular Baptists turned to high Calvinism, so emphasizing the sovereignty of God that they saw no need for evangelism. From the middle years of the century, however, the Evangelical Revival brought new life to the churches and the birth of the modern Protestant mission movement. Andrew Fuller and William Carey led the renewal and missionary outreach among Particular Baptists, a new body of General Baptists was formed, and Robert and James Haldane advanced Baptist work in Scotland.

The nineteenth century witnessed a flourishing of Baptist work in the British Isles. Baptist unions were organized in Great Britain (1813), Wales (1866), Scotland (1869), and Ireland (1895); they coordinated the work of individual congregations. In 1891, the General and Particular Baptists united in the Baptist Union of Great Britain and Ireland. Baptists participated in moral reform movements (temperance, gambling, Sunday observance) as well as in social issues (slavery in the colonies, education for everyone, urban poverty, and unemployment). They formed colleges to train ministers and started Sunday schools to reach young people. Great Baptist preachers of the Victorian age, Charles Haddon Spurgeon, Alexander Maclaren, and John Clifford, among others, inspired people at home and abroad. Some differences, however, among British Baptists continue to the present day over such matters as open membership, ministry of women, ecumenical relationships, and certain theological beliefs.

The first Baptist churches in America were in the New England colonies, to which many Puritans had emigrated. Soon after arriving in

Baptists: A Global Community of Faith

Boston in 1631, Puritan minister Roger Williams adopted Separatist views. Forced to leave Massachusetts Bay, he founded the colony of Providence (present-day Rhode Island) in 1636 with complete freedom in religious matters. Two years later, he was baptized and formed the first Baptist church in America but remained a Baptist pastor for only a short time. He is chiefly remembered for his stirring writings on religious liberty.

Shortly afterwards, Dr. John Clarke left Boston for Rhode Island, where he joined Williams in the struggle for religious freedom. He established a congregation that was clearly Baptist in doctrine and polity. In 1651, Baptist Obadiah Holmes was publicly whipped in Boston for participating with Clarke in a home prayer meeting, and Henry Dunster, the second president of Harvard College (now University), lost his job in 1654 for affirming believer's baptism. A Baptist church was formed in Boston in 1665. Its members were persecuted for several years; they drafted the first Baptist confession of faith in the American colonies.

By the 1690s, congregations existed in South Carolina and Pennsylvania. Aided by the enthusiasm flowing from the first Great Awakening, the revival that swept the colonies in the mid-eighteenth century, Baptists soon became more numerous. The Philadelphia Association was formed in 1707, the Charleston in 1751, and others in New England, the Middle Colonies, and the South. In 1781, the first church west of the Appalachian Mountains was organized in Kentucky. Eighteenth-century Baptists were diverse; the main groups were the Regular Baptists, the General or Free Will Baptists, the revivalistic Separate Baptists, and the Seventh-Day Baptists.

THE STRUGGLE FOR RELIGIOUS LIBERTY

Although some Baptists had misgivings about the War for American Independence (1775–1783), most saw it as a war for freedom, which for them meant religious freedom. Isaac Backus, originally a New Light Congregationalist minister, was converted in the Great Awakening and became a leader of the newly emerging Separate Baptists. He wrote pamphlets criticizing taxation for religious purposes and affirming liberty of conscience. The Warren Baptist Association in Massachusetts sent him to the First Continental Congress in 1774 to argue the case for ending religious establishments;

WE BAPTISTS

and when the War for American Independence broke out, he supported the American cause. As Backus later said, he and his brethren fought on two fronts: against British troops for civil liberty and against Massachusetts legislators for religious liberty. He helped to secure his state's ratification of the U.S. Constitution in 1789, but religious liberty was not achieved until 1833 when Massachusetts gave up its religious establishment.

In colonial Virginia, Baptists were frequently jailed for preaching, and they lobbied the legislature for religious liberty. The grievances of this "heretical" sect were ignored until their support for the War for American Independence, and their request to send chaplains for the soldiers helped to change the public's perception of them. They also formed a coalition with Thomas Jefferson, James Madison, and others who also wished to disestablish the Church of England (now becoming the Protestant Episcopal Church), and they achieved that in Virginia through the Statute for Establishing Religious Freedom (1786). Later, Virginia Baptists, led by John Leland and others, persuaded Madison to include a firm guarantee of religious liberty in the amendments to the U.S. Constitution known as the Bill of Rights. Hence, the First Amendment opens as follows: "Congress shall make no law respecting an establishment of religion, or prohibiting the free exercise thereof."

After becoming president of the United States, Jefferson clarified the meaning of this statement in response to a request from the Danbury (Connecticut) Baptist Association, which had been unable to persuade its state legislature to end the Congregationalist establishment there and had asked the president for his opinion. Jefferson replied in a letter (1802) to them that religion is a matter between man and God and that government has no power to regulate such matters. The First Amendment built a wall of separation between church and state.

Many regard this principle as the new nation's greatest contribution to civilization. It clearly opened the way for unparalleled Baptist growth in the United States. Unlike Britain, where Baptists consumed much of their energy in combating discriminatory laws preventing involvement in public life and requiring monetary support of Anglican parishes, and unlike other European countries in which the official churches persecuted Baptists, Americans were unhindered in following God's call to preach the gospel. The separation of church and state enabled them to evangelize freely.

Baptists: A Global Community of Faith

BAPTIST GROWTH IN THE UNITED STATES

Although Baptists had no national organization, they quickly embarked upon mission, beginning with the Massachusetts Baptist Missionary Society, founded in 1802, which endeavored to follow the settlers westward and found churches in their midst. Such remarkable pioneers as John Mason Peck and Isaac McCoy worked among pioneers on the frontier in the Ohio and Mississippi River valleys and ministered to the Indian populations as well.

The hope of a national Baptist body seemed to be fulfilled with the formation in Philadelphia in 1814 of a foreign mission society, the General Missionary Convention of the Baptist Denomination in the United States of America for Foreign Missions, called the Triennial Convention because it met every three years. Luther Rice, who had gone with Adoniram and Ann Judson to Burma in 1812, returned home to develop a support system. The Triennial Convention began to engage in new church development and educational enterprises at home as well as in foreign missions, but Rice's fund-raising methods and the founding of societies not directly accountable to local congregations engendered opposition. This divisive anti-mission movement, marked by a tenacious localism and a strong sense of Calvinistic predestination, became the Anti-Mission, Hardshell, or Primitive Baptists.

By 1824, the Triennial Convention had reverted to a single-purpose society to foster foreign missions. Other voluntary societies promoted tract distribution, Sunday schools, and home missions, and numerous Baptist colleges were opened across the country. Local churches and associations began to organize state conventions, and these provided another type of connectional relationship for the churches.

The sectional disagreements over slavery, however, led to a widening gap between Baptists in the North and the South. In 1845, the Southern Baptist Convention (SBC) was formed, the first truly comprehensive Baptist organization in America. Although it reflected the decentralization characteristic of Baptists, the SBC began by emphasizing the associational principle, as opposed to the voluntary society approach, and developed its own boards that were supported by the churches.

During the nineteenth century, Landmarkism was a disruptive force in the SBC. This system of beliefs taught the unbroken succession of Baptist churches since the New Testament age, the absolute independence of local congregations, closed communion, the refusal to recognize

WE BAPTISTS

baptisms by immersion performed by non-Baptists, and opposition to cooperative ventures such as mission boards or societies, viewing them as unbiblical.

In the North and the West, voluntary societies provided the connectional link among Baptists even as they organized state conventions and ethnic associations. The Baptist General Tract Society, founded in 1824 and later known as the American Baptist Publication and Sunday School Society (ABPS), engaged in educational work. The American Baptist Home Mission Society (ABHMS, 1832) worked among immigrant groups and frontier settlers; after the Civil War (1861–1865), it also served among freed blacks in the South and Indians in the West. Following the break in 1845, the Triennial Convention was renamed the American Baptist Missionary Union (ABMU, after 1910 the American Baptist Foreign Mission Society—ABFMS) and functioned as the North's chief missionary sending agency.

Women's societies also supported the missionary endeavor. The Women's American Baptist Foreign Mission Society (1871) was led by such dynamic individuals as Lucy Peabody and Helen Barrett Montgomery. Woman's Missionary Union (1888), an auxiliary of the SBC, was inspired by the courageous missionary to China, Charlotte (Lottie) Diggs Moon, and led by Annie Armstrong. The annual Lottie Moon Christmas Offering has received more than one billion dollars for missions.

In 1907 Baptist leaders in the North and the West, finding that the voluntary societies did not provide an adequate basis for unity, formed the Northern Baptist Convention (NBC). The separate societies became boards, and the convention structure was similar to that of the SBC. The NBC has been involved in the Ecumenical Movement from its beginning. The Swedish-American and German-American Baptists went their separate ways and eventually formed their own denominations, the Baptist General Conference and North American Baptist Conference.

The emergence of biblical criticism and theological liberalism caused deep divisions among Baptists on both sides of the Atlantic. Charles H. Spurgeon in England announced that liberalism was creeping into the churches, and the Down Grade controversy he launched shook the Baptist Union and influenced many Baptists overseas as well. In the United States in both North and South, new ideas, particularly the concept of social Christianity espoused by Baptist professors Walter Rauschenbusch and Shailer Mathews, caused dissension. After World War I, the Fundamentalist-Modernist controversy tore at the fabric of the NBC, leading to the secession of many conservatives and the formation of the

Baptists: A Global Community of Faith

General Association of Regular Baptist Churches (1932) and the Conservative Baptist Association of America (1947).

Similar schisms occurred in the South led by J. Frank Norris and other fundamentalists, and these resulted in the creation of independent Baptist churches and some new groups, the most noteworthy being the Baptist Bible Fellowship International (1950). Also, two significant Landmark denominations were formed during these years: the American Baptist Association (1924) and the Baptist Missionary Association (1950).

After World War II, the NBC restructured itself as the American Baptist Convention (1950) and then as American Baptist Churches U.S.A. (ABC, 1972) and greatly broadened its outreach to racial minorities. Through an effective home mission program, the SBC moved from a regional to a national body and became the largest Protestant denomination in North America. Also, many large independent Baptist churches, staunchly fundamentalist in their orientation, existed apart from the various Baptist conventions. A fundamentalist-moderate controversy radically affected SBC life in the 1980s and 1990s, resulting in the formation of new Baptist organizations and in a restructuring of the SBC.

Blacks (African Americans) now make up almost a quarter of the Baptist population in the United States. Their churches have been intimately linked with the struggle from slavery to freedom and are social institutions which provide blacks with identity and support. These churches were the first and, for a long time, the only institutions that blacks controlled as their own. Initially, many slaves became Christians and joined the Baptist churches of their masters, but the first African Baptist church was organized in Savannah, Georgia, in 1788. By 1800, there were ten black churches in the South. In the North free blacks had more opportunity to establish congregations; in 1840, they formed a national organization to which forty-eight churches belonged by 1865. By the time of the Civil War, some 205 black churches existed, but a majority of blacks were still members of multiracial churches controlled by whites.

Black Baptist church formation increased greatly in the South after 1865. Numerous associations and state conventions were formed, and the Baptist Foreign Missionary Convention of the USA was organized in 1880 to foster missionary work in Africa. This convention and two other agencies united in 1895 to form the National Baptist Convention, USA, Inc. Schisms due to non-theological causes resulted in the formation of four other black Baptist conventions: Lott Carey Baptist Foreign Mission

WE BAPTISTS

Convention, USA (1897), National Baptist Convention of America (1915), Progressive National Baptist Convention, Inc. (1961), and National Missionary Baptist Convention of America (1988).

Many black churches today are dually aligned with the ABC or SBC, thus making precise membership figures hard to determine. Black Baptist pastors also played a key role in the Civil Rights movement of the 1950s and 1960s, with Martin Luther King Jr., a Baptist preacher, universally recognized as a major figure of the twentieth century.

THE SPREAD OUTWARD

From Britain and the United States, the Baptist message was carried to the British settlement colonies, continental Europe, Asia, Africa, and Latin America. The first churches in Canada were planted in Nova Scotia in the 1760s, and the Great Awakening in the Atlantic provinces fostered the spread of Baptist teachings. Also, some black Baptists moved northward and formed churches. Scottish Baptists and U.S. missionaries founded churches in Ontario and Quebec, but within a few years the Canadians themselves were spreading the gospel across their vast country. Regionalism, missionary work within Canada, and immigration from Europe all contributed to the complexity of Canadian Baptist development. A network of Baptist denominations grew up over the years, the largest of which are the Canadian Baptist Federation (now Canadian Baptist Ministries) and the Fellowship of Evangelical Baptist Churches in Canada.

The British government in South Africa in the 1820s brought the Albany Settlers to the Eastern Cape, and the Baptist families among them organized the first church in Grahamstown. When the authorities granted land to German immigrants in the 1850s, Baptists from Germany started some churches in this community. The two groups formed a Baptist Union in 1877 and reached out to the Dutch-speaking (Afrikaans) and Indian peoples. To work among the black population, the union created the South African Baptist Missionary Society, which in 1927 organized a separate Bantu Baptist Church and in 1966 the Baptist Convention of South Africa. Due to the widening gap over apartheid issues and cultural differences, the largely black convention declared its independence from the union in 1987. Efforts toward reconciliation of the two bodies are proceeding.

More than forty years passed after the British arrival in Australia before the first Baptist meeting occurred. In 1831, the Scot John McKeag

Baptists: A Global Community of Faith

began a ministry in Sydney, but it soon collapsed. The disheartened remnant asked the Baptist Missionary Society to send out a worker, and John Saunders arrived in 1834. Under his leadership a church was organized and the image of the Baptists enhanced. In 1835, Henry Dowling launched a Baptist work in Hobart, Tasmania, and the first services were held in Adelaide and Melbourne in 1837. The first Baptist congregation in Queensland was formed in 1855 and in Western Australia in 1895.

Baptists in Australia faced great difficulties. The vast distances made coordination difficult. Baptist life in the various regions developed more or less independently, but soon Baptists in each state formed associations or unions to promote ministerial training, missions at home and abroad, educational enterprises, and charitable works. In 1926, they organized the Baptist Union of Australia. Although creating a distinct Australian identity proved to be difficult, the main unifying force among Baptists has been overseas missionary work, with significant outreach especially in Papua New Guinea.

As in Australia, Baptist work in New Zealand started slowly, with the first congregation founded in 1851. Three decades later, twenty-two churches organized the Baptist Union of New Zealand to foster unity and church growth. The union has sponsored foreign missions, evangelism, and theological education. Important today is multicultural work among the aboriginal Maori and immigrant Asians and Pacific Islanders. Both Australian and New Zealand Baptists are conservative evangelicals in their faith but not fundamentalists, and many churches have adopted charismatic worship styles.

ACROSS THE EUROPEAN CONTINENT

Both British and American influences assisted in Baptist expansion in Europe. Both eighteenth-century Pietism, which had attracted many people on the European continent, and the nineteenth-century Awakening stressed a more personal, devotional, Bible-centered life. The result was Bible study and prayer groups that traveling Baptist evangelists discovered or gathered together.

The most influential Continental evangelist was Johann Gerhard Oncken. Born in Germany and apprenticed to a Scottish merchant who took him to Britain, he was converted in a Methodist chapel. Then the Continental Society for the Diffusion of Religious Knowledge sent him to Hamburg, Germany, to engage in evangelism and tract distribution.

11

WE BAPTISTS

Dissatisfied with conditions in the established Lutheran church, he considered the idea of a church comprised only of believers and found this to be biblical. Oncken contacted Barnas Sears, an American Baptist theological professor in Germany on study leave, who came to Hamburg, baptized him and six others in the Elbe River in 1834, and ordained him the pastor of a new Baptist church.

Oncken quickly established ties with the Triennial Convention, which appointed him as its agent and provided him with funds to support other workers in Germany. He traveled incessantly in his country and elsewhere and gathered born-again Christians into congregations based on believer's baptism. He also journeyed to England and America on fundraising trips.

Oncken's missionary understanding of the priesthood of all believers impacted European Baptists. His famous phrase, "Every Baptist a missionary," challenged many young men to follow his example. After he had won numerous skilled craftsmen to Christ, they traveled around Europe as journeymen working in their trades and spreading the gospel. Soon, several congregations existed in Germany and Denmark, and Oncken formed a Baptist union in 1849. He also created in Hamburg a training institute for lay evangelists which evolved into a seminary.

As evangelists went out from Germany, churches were formed in Switzerland, the Austro-Hungarian Empire, Poland, Lithuania, Latvia, Estonia, Romania, and Bulgaria. Although always under pressure, the churches in these countries grew and survived, even under Communist dictatorships. The German Baptists also thrived, but the Nazi regime (1933–1945) pressured them to unite with other small bodies to form the Union of Evangelical Free Churches, which remains their formal title.

American influence was strong in Sweden. Frederick O. Nilsson was a Swedish sailor who became a Christian in New York and returned to his native land as a missionary of the Seamen's Friend Society. In Göteborg, he met a sailor who won him to the Baptist position. Oncken baptized Nilsson in Hamburg, and he formed the first Baptist congregation in Sweden in 1848. Nilsson baptized Anders Wiberg, who later became the great Swedish Baptist leader. After Wiberg went to the United States and worked for the ABPS, he returned in 1855 with ABPS support, pastored the Baptist church in Stockholm, and wrote the first Swedish Baptist confession of faith.

In Russia and Ukraine, the Tsarist government allowed German-speaking evangelists to preach and form congregations among the Germans who had settled there and granted their churches legal recognition in 1879.

12

Baptists: A Global Community of Faith

They maintained close ties with Hamburg; Oncken even visited them twice. But the authorities regarded ethnic Russians, Ukrainians, and Byelorussians as Russian Orthodox and strictly prohibited their conversion to other confessions.

In spite of official opposition, an evangelical movement developed in the Ukraine, and in 1868–1870 the first ethnic Ukrainians were baptized. In 1863, in Tiflis, Georgia (Caucasus region), a German Baptist won to Christ the Russian merchant Nikita Voronin, who, in turn, formed a congregation. Voronin's leading convert was Vassily Pavlov, whom he baptized and sent to Hamburg for training and ordination. Through Pavlov's missionary work, the Baptists grew in numbers despite persecution, and the movements in the Ukraine and Caucasus joined together in 1884 as the Russian Baptist Union. Meanwhile, Ivan Prokhanov, an engineer in St. Petersburg, became a Baptist and founded the Union of Evangelical Christians in 1908, but the two bodies could not get together.

The Soviet government in the 1930s so persecuted all churches that Baptists almost disappeared, but Josef Stalin, wanting their support in the war against Nazi Germany, permitted those surviving in the two bodies to merge in 1944 as the Union of Evangelical Christians-Baptists. The freedom granted was very limited, and the Baptists split over whether to cooperate with the government by registering their churches. Since the Soviet Union dissolved in 1991, Baptists in the successor states have formed separate unions and are vigorously evangelizing.

INTO ALL THE WORLD—THE MISSIONARY ADVANCE

The Baptist message began to move out from Britain and North America in the 1780s. William Carey, a young shoemaker in Northamptonshire, England, was baptized in 1783 and became a self-educated preacher. He had a brilliant mind and a burning desire to evangelize the lost. In *An Enquiry into the Obligations of Christians to Use Means for Conversion of the Heathens* (1792), he urged his fellow Particular Baptist ministers to support a foreign mission enterprise. Christ's command to go into all the world is as binding as that to baptize, and the program to accomplish this is simple: pray, plan, pay. His "deathless sermon" on the theme, "Expect great things from God; attempt great things for God," moved his hearers to found the Baptist Missionary Society (BMS) in 1792, and the following year Carey and John Thomas sailed to India.

WE BAPTISTS

At Serampore, near Calcutta, Carey translated the Bible, composed grammars and dictionaries, set up a printing press, and opened a training college. The BMS developed a support system, dispatched more missionaries to India, and expanded its work into other nations.

The BMS was active in the states of West Bengal and Bihar and in Delhi, whereas the General Baptist Missionary Society of England opened work in the state of Orissa (1822). Both struggled against the caste system. The BMS mission to Mizoram in the northeast (1903) witnessed more converts. Since 1970, more than half of the churches have entered the Church of North India.

Missionaries of the Triennial Convention began to work in Andhra Pradesh with its Telugu-speaking people in 1836, and today the Samavesam of Telugu Baptist Churches has 475,000 members. Also in 1836, missionaries of the Triennial Convention started a mission in Assam in the northeast and soon expanded into Nagaland and Manipur. They reduced the tribal languages to writing and established schools. Baptists became very numerous in these states. In 1950, the Council of Baptist Churches of North East India was formed, but today the five regional conventions are becoming more important. About 550,000 Baptists are to be found in the northeast.

In 1874, the Baptists of Ontario and Quebec sent missionaries to northern Andhra Pradesh, and as a consequence today the Convention of Baptist Churches of the Northern Circars has 126,000 members. Today, there are more Baptists in India, about 1.7 million, than any nation other than the United States, and the Baptists are the most numerous Protestant denomination in India.

Baptist work in the Caribbean began before the end of the eighteenth century. In the Bahamas the first church emerged during the 1780s, the BMS sent its first missionaries in 1833, and a union was formed in 1892. The founder of Baptist work in Jamaica, George Leile, had been a slave in America; after securing his freedom, he went to Kingston and in 1783 formed a Baptist church. The BMS sent its first missionary in 1814; another, William Knibb, mobilized British Baptists against slavery and helped to persuade Parliament to pass the Emancipation Act (1833). The Jamaicans set up their own mission agency, which in cooperation with the BMS sent missionaries to Africa in 1843, and formed the Jamaica Baptist Union in 1849. Baptist work in French-speaking Haiti was sporadic after the first church was formed in 1836, despite the labor of missionaries from the BMS and from the Jamaican Baptist Missionary Society. But after the advent of the ABFMS

Baptists: A Global Community of Faith

in 1923, there was great growth; the Baptist Convention of Haiti was constituted in 1964.

Baptists in America were keenly interested in Carey's work and gave money to support it. In 1810, six theological students, including Adoniram Judson and Luther Rice, petitioned the Congregational church association in Massachusetts to send them to Burma. It agreed to form the American Board of Commissioners for Foreign Missions (ABCFM), which in 1812 appointed Judson and his wife Ann Hasseltine, Rice, and three others. On the voyage to India, Judson studied the question of believer's baptism and became convinced of its correctness. In Calcutta the Judsons and Rice were immersed and resigned from the ABCFM. Judson went on to Burma, where he and Ann carried on pioneer missionary work under the most difficult circumstances. Rice returned home to secure funding, with the result that the Triennial Convention was organized in 1814. This agency sent more missionaries to Burma, and remarkable growth occurred. In present-day Myanmar, Baptists number more than half a million.

The African Baptist Missionary Society, formed in 1815 in Richmond, Virginia, as an auxiliary of the Triennial Convention, appointed Lott Carey and Collin Teague in 1819 to serve in Liberia, and they formed in Richmond and took to Monrovia the first Baptist congregation on the African continent. Other missionary agencies supplied personnel, and today there are about sixty thousand Liberian Baptists.

The BMS expanded into Africa in 1843 when Alfred Saker entered Cameroon. It established a station in Angola in 1879 and one in the Congo in 1880. Under the leadership of the remarkable explorer-missionary George Grenfell, the BMS gained a firm foothold in the Congo basin. Soon the ABFMS came, and within a few decades a thriving community was present. The various Baptist groups in the independent Democratic Republic of Congo now have more than 750,000 members. In Cameroon, where first German Baptists and later the Paris Evangelical Missionary Society supplied missionaries, Baptists now number more than 180,000. In 1960, the BMS separated its work in Angola from that in Congo; there are now about 115,000 Baptists in Angola.

In 1846, the SBC's Foreign Mission Board (FMB) chose China as its first mission field. J. Lewis Shuck, its first missionary, after serving under the Triennial Convention in Macao, moved in 1842 to Hong Kong, where he organized the first Baptist church on Chinese soil. Later, he labored in Canton. Effective missionaries such as Roswell H. Graves and Matthew T. Yates soon followed. The SBC-FMB, the ABMU, and the BMS developed

WE BAPTISTS

extensive missionary work in China until the advent of the Communist regime (1949). Both Hong Kong and Taiwan have become centers of missionary activity among displaced Chinese.

At the outbreak of the American Civil War, the SBC-FMB was supporting twenty-four African-American missionaries in Africa. Among these was Thomas J. Bowen, who not only opened the work in Nigeria in 1850 but also compiled the first Yoruba language dictionary. Internal problems and tribal opposition hindered the Baptist cause; but by the 1930s, unity had returned and unprecedented growth had begun. Schools and hospitals were established and became effective means of evangelization. Today, the Nigerian Baptist Convention reports a million church members.

Romanian Baptists derive from a German congregation formed in Bucharest in 1863 and a Hungarian church constituted in Transylvania in 1875. Forming a union in 1919, Romanian Baptists were aided by SBC-FMB missionaries between the two world wars and suffered at the hands of the government both before and during World War II and under the Communist regime. Numbering today about one hundred thousand, they are aggressively evangelizing.

In Mexico the first Baptist church was formed in Monterey in 1864 by a Baptist colporteur of the American Bible Society. Both the ABHMS and the SBC-FMB sent numerous missionaries, and a national Baptist convention was organized in 1903. But political revolution (1910–1917) brought repression. Today, Mexican Baptists number 120,000.

The first Baptist church in Japan was constituted in Yokohama in 1873 by ABMU missionaries. SBC-FMB missionaries began work on the island of Kyushu in 1892. Forced to become a part of the United Church of Christ in Japan during World War II, these Baptists subsequently formed separate Baptist bodies. Growth has been slow but steady, and yet the fourteen Baptist bodies report fewer than fifty-thousand members.

The SBC-FMB sent to Brazil in 1881 William B. and Anne Bagby, who were joined the next year by Zachary and Kate Taylor. These couples organized a church in Salvador, Bahia, and shortly thereafter a church in Rio de Janeiro. William Bagby spent fifty-eight years in missionary service, and his wife sixty-one. All five of their children became missionaries, four of whom served in Brazil. These pioneers, together with Erik and Ida Nelson in the Amazon Valley, laid strong foundations. As converts formed churches, the churches then organized associations and conventions—for example, the Brazilian Baptist Convention was formed in 1907, with boards similar to those of the SBC. Other Baptist bodies in

Baptists: A Global Community of Faith

Great Britain, the U.S., and Sweden began missionary work in Brazil during the twentieth century. Vigorous evangelism, numerous schools, publication work, social ministries, strict church discipline, and home and foreign missionary support have characterized Baptists in Brazil, who today are organized in fourteen different bodies and number about 1.2 million.

The Argentine Baptist pioneer was Paul Besson, Swiss-born, French-speaking former Reformed Church minister who entered Argentina as a Baptist missionary in 1881, organized a church in Buenos Aires, and led in the struggle for religious freedom. The first SBC-FMB missionary, Sidney M. Sowell, arrived in 1903, and a convention was formed in 1908. Argentine Baptists today number about sixty thousand.

Baptist work in Korea between 1889 and 1949 did not have the name Baptist, it being interdenominational and evangelical. This body invited the SBC-FMB to send missionaries, and John and Jewell Abernathy arrived in 1950. Confined to South Korea, the Korean Baptist Convention, despite a temporary schism, and with emphasis on prayer, theological education, and evangelization, has had significant growth, today reporting about 650,000 members.

Malawi Baptists derive from the labors of Joseph Booth, an English Baptist who, after arriving in Nyasaland in 1892, established industrial missions and encouraged the National Baptist Convention, USA, and the Seventh Day Baptists in the U.S. to send missionaries. Today, seven Baptist bodies report about 190,000 members.

The presence of Baptists in the Philippines postdates the Spanish-American War (1898). Eric Lund, a Swede serving under the ABMU, opened a mission on the island of Panay in 1900. The Association of Baptists for World Evangelism established a church in Manila in 1928. The SBC-FMB, with the closing of China, began to send missionaries in 1948, especially to Mindinao. Almost every Baptist sending agency in the U.S. now has representatives in the Philippines, and nineteen Baptist bodies report about 315,000 members.

Other nations having sizable Baptist communities today had their Baptist beginnings during the twentieth century: Zambia, assisted by South African, Australian, and Free Swedish missionaries and later by SBC-FMB; Central African Republic, with Baptist Mid-Missions and the Örebro Mission (Sweden) as the sending bodies; Zimbabwe, whose missionaries were first German Baptists from South Africa and later SBC-FMB missionaries; Mozambique, aided by missionaries from Sweden and Portugal; Rwanda, helped by Danish Baptist missionaries

WE BAPTISTS

and the Conservative Baptist Foreign Mission Society; Indonesia, where SBC-FMB missionaries, formerly in China, opened work in 1951, though a German, Gottlob Bruckner, had pioneered in the nineteenth century; and Kenya and Tanzania, where SBC-FMB missionaries began to work in 1956.

In nearly all of these nations, Baptist church life is under national leadership, and foreign missionaries work fraternally with the nationally led Baptist bodies. During the last quarter of the twentieth century, Baptist conventions and unions outside Great Britain and North America have begun to send their own foreign missionaries. Today, at least twenty-nine such unions and conventions are supporting at least 1,042 foreign missionaries. The largest sending bodies are the Brazilian Baptist Convention with 445 missionaries and the Korean Baptist Convention with 220.

THE BAPTIST WORLD ALLIANCE

Baptist bodies are found nearly everywhere in the world, and their numbers increase steadily. But Baptists need to know one another better, to encourage each other's ministries and missions, and to cooperate in the struggle for religious freedom. These are the purposes of the BWA. Formed in 1905, it has nearly two hundred member bodies throughout the world, representing more than three-fourths of all Baptists. Through its commissions, committees, and workgroups, the BWA engages in evangelism, disaster relief, development aid, study and research, defense of human rights, and sharing of common concerns. Although separated in numerous ethnic, national, and denominational bodies, Baptists share a common commitment to a biblical faith, the Lordship of Jesus Christ, and religious freedom. Baptists are indeed a global community, and the BWA exists to encourage and help them to fulfill Christ's mission to the world.

CHAPTER TWO

What Baptists Believe

AS WE FACE THE END OF THIS CENTURY AND MILLENNIUM, WE are bound to ask: Does it really matter what Baptists believe? In many parts of the world, confident prophets are predicting the end of denominations as we have known them. But significant advances in understanding between denominations and exciting experiments in sharing across traditional boundaries do not detract from the importance of knowing the Baptist story. A concern for unity is not advanced by ignoring biblical truths which denominations have preserved. Issues relating to theological truth are always important. To know Baptist beliefs is both to recognize what some of God's people have been willing to die for and to appreciate what Baptists bring to new relationships emerging among churches today. There are many signs that the Baptist view of the church is gaining acceptance.

For Baptists, then, to understand their beliefs is to recall their distinctive mix of emphases in faith and practice, rather than to claim any beliefs as being absolutely unique. Knowing our beliefs enables us Baptists to affirm what we hold with other Christians and to discern what distinctively marks our way of being church. The question is important because it helps us to know who we are, reminds us of rich resources available to us, gives a focus to help us in time of rapid change, and assists us in exploring the contribution we may make to the coming of the kingdom of God in our day.

WE BAPTISTS

What is important is that we ask what Baptists believe with humility and in a spirit of openness to the future and to further insights. At their best, Baptists have shown a significant way of being Christian, being church, and living in the world.

DISCOVERING WHAT BAPTISTS BELIEVE

Such a task is more complicated than we might first think. There is no central body, such as the Roman Catholic Vatican, which defines what Baptists believe. There is no one historic formulation of beliefs, such as the Anglican Thirty-nine Articles or the Augsburg Confession of Lutherans, which all Baptists at some given moment in time have affirmed. There is no one historic person, such as Martin Luther for the Lutherans or John Calvin for the Reformed churches, whose teaching gives to Baptists their basic legacy of beliefs.

How, then, can anyone say what Baptists believe? The answer derives from history and present experience. Knowledge of the Baptist heritage, such as introduced earlier in this book, enables us to begin to form an answer to our question. Certain individuals and groups sought to be faithful and obedient Christians in what were troubled times for Christians. The churches that emerged from those struggles valued freedom to be God's people above all else. They did not hesitate to prepare confessions of faith which interpreted and explained their beliefs, but they refused to confer any final authority on those statements. Rather, the confessions authentically identified Baptist beliefs for non-Baptists and served internally as guidelines for fellowship and teaching. These historic confessions are of basic importance for us in our quest, but so too are contemporary statements by representative Baptists, such as those prepared by the Baptist Heritage Commission of the Baptist World Alliance (BWA) in 1989 or by the European Baptist Federation in 1993.

This means that it is possible to summarize what Baptists believe today, but, as freedom is a fundamental belief for all true Baptists, we will not be surprised to learn that there is considerable diversity among Baptists as to the details of these beliefs. Baptist unions or conventions in different countries and states ordinarily prepare summary statements as a guide to their member churches and to other interested Christians. These certainly reveal differences, but in the mainstream of Baptist beliefs, such as among those bodies which are members of the BWA, there is remarkable agreement

What Baptists Believe

about Baptist distinctives. Indeed, that agreement is often greater in reality than that found among denominations which do have a common authority figure or a creedal symbol of their faith.

BELIEFS SHARED WITH OTHER CHRISTIANS

Recalling the historical origins of the Baptist movement also enables us to make some basic affirmations about what Baptists believe. In the first place, Baptists share the most fundamental beliefs with all other Christians. These begin with belief in the triune God who is Father, Son, and Holy Spirit. This eternal God is the Creator of all things. Human beings, being tempted, fell into sin and out of fellowship with God. Jesus is the unique, incarnate Son of God, being also fully man, who died for our sins, rose again from the grave on the third day, and ascended to heaven, there to make intercession for his people. Those who trust in him become part of his church, being sealed by the Holy Spirit for eternal salvation, and Christ himself will one day appear in glory to consummate human history and bring in fully the reign of God.

Thus, Baptists understand themselves as sharing in the beliefs of the earliest Christian church as expressed in the New Testament. They also affirm the central teachings of the sixteenth-century Reformers, who set out to renew the faith and life of the church. In particular, they follow in the footsteps of the more radical wing of the Reformation, including the Anabaptists on the continent of Europe and the English Puritans and Separatists of the seventeenth century. All held that we are justified by God's grace through faith alone and that neither priest nor church stands between God and the individual Christian. All accepted the Scriptures as the final written authority for all matters of faith and practice. All stressed the importance of the church within the purposes of God. In particular, Baptists had a strong belief in the presence of the risen Christ with his covenanted people to guide their life.

BAPTIST DISTINCTIVES

While sharing with all Protestants a belief in the authority of the Bible, Baptists have shown a strong commitment to the supremacy of that authority, greater than that of any creedal formulation or any church leader. Their agreement with Separatists that a church's

21

membership should consist only of committed disciples in a covenant relationship led them to the further insistence that baptism was only for believers and that this baptism helped to safeguard the church as a fellowship of believers only. This was their most radical practice in the eyes of their contemporaries and led them to be linked with the Anabaptists (literally, "Re-baptizers") and eventually to be nicknamed "Baptists." For the Baptists, believer's baptism has been a strong expression of their faithful obedience to the Scriptures and their determination to be the Lord's free people in every way revealed to them, no matter what the cost.

When we claim that Baptist principles include the supreme authority of the Bible, the nature of the church as a fellowship of believers, baptism for believers only, and complete religious freedom, what we mean is that at one time or another Baptists felt that one or more of these truths was being obscured or distorted by the contemporary church. By their insistence upon these truths, Baptists became a separate movement. Their conclusions seemed to them to be the inevitable result of the principles of the Reformation, especially of the supreme authority of the Scriptures. No one doctrine is exclusive to Baptists, but no other group has maintained emphases on all these points in this particular way.

The following outline of Baptist beliefs is intended to be descriptive of what, according to general agreement, Baptists *do believe*. In no sense could it be prescriptive of what Baptist *should believe*. At every point, Baptists will want to be true to what the Scriptures teach, although differences of interpretation or judgment on issues about which the Scriptures do not seem to speak inevitably lead to some differences among Baptists. Wherever possible, these differences will be noted.

The Kingdom of God

One helpful approach is to begin where, according to the Gospels, Jesus began, namely, with the proclamation of the kingdom of God (Mark 1:15). Baptists share gladly in the joyful recognition of the sovereignty of the living God who has come to us in Jesus. As we receive the good news about Jesus, we are born again and enter into that kingdom (John 3:5). This gospel is central to our identity and mission. The church as the community of faith is a sign and witness of that gracious rule of God which extends to every facet of life, but the church must never be equated with the sovereign rule. Baptists, along with all of God's people, are primarily called to be loyal to the kingdom of God and the costly

What Baptists Believe

discipleship which it demands. This gives us a mission of reconciliation that reaches to every person, every nation, every human institution, and indeed the created order.

Baptists from their earliest times have focused upon the way that this rule of God is mediated through the living presence of Christ among his people. The origin of the church is in the Christian gospel, which created and renews the church in every age. This gospel ("good news") of the kingdom of God centers in Jesus Christ as Lord, is known through the Scriptures, and is made effective by the Holy Spirit. To think about these affirmations will lead us to understand the Baptist doctrine of the church and its mission.

The Lordship of Jesus Christ

All Christians confess that Jesus is Lord (Rom. 10:9). Baptists insist that the life and structures of the church should affirm the Lordship of Christ. No form of church or state authority should be permitted to distort this truth. Baptists have always sought to uphold the sole and exclusive authority of Jesus Christ.

It is worth recalling the witness of Menno Simons, sixteenth-century Anabaptist leader. At a time of dramatic change in the Christian world, when literally hundreds of his friends were being killed for their desire to live as Christians and to form churches according to the Bible as they read it, Menno took the following text as his motto, and it appeared on everything that he wrote: "For no one can lay any foundation other than the one already laid, which is Jesus Christ" (1 Cor. 3:11, NIV).

Baptists, too, affirm above all else that Jesus Christ, the living Son of God, known in Scripture and in the experience of God's people by his Spirit, is the center of our being as a church. He is the supreme authority for our life together.

The Authority of the Scriptures

Baptists believe that the Bible is both the true record of God's revelation to our world and the supreme written guide for our faith and practice today. Because it leads us to Jesus Christ the living Word, we speak of the Bible as "the Word of God," and believe it was inspired by God's Spirit. Baptists reflect different views about the mode of the Bible's inspiration, but all regard it as totally sufficient; that is, all teaching must be in harmony with the Scriptures, and all teaching must be tested by the Scriptures only.

Of course, there are differences concerning interpretation. Although Baptists accept help from those qualified to interpret the Bible's language,

23

WE BAPTISTS

literature, and culture, and recognize the guidance given by responsible spiritual teachers to the community of the faithful, no one can interpret dogmatically for another. Baptists believe that the church will be constantly renewed as the Scriptures are heard and also affirm, as one of the Pilgrim Fathers, John Robinson, declared, that "the Lord had more light and truth yet to break forth out of his Holy Word" ("Parting Advice"). Because of their belief in the final written authority of the Scriptures, Baptists have not normally imposed any confessional statement or creed upon an individual church member. Doctrinal statements do, however, stand as testimonies to our belief and often guide ventures in which churches cooperate.

The Work of the Holy Spirit

The same Spirit who inspired the Scriptures guides believers today as they hear and interpret the Word. The Holy Spirit enables the church to hear the Scriptures afresh and so to be renewed in every generation, while also making the proclamation of the gospel effective in the life of an individual believer. The Holy Spirit convicts us of sin and leads us through conversion, working in us to produce a new person conforming to the image of Christ and producing appropriate fruit in our lives. This presence of the Spirit is personal but never individualistic, for the Spirit draws believers together into the community of faith and endows God's people with spiritual gifts *(charismata)* for their worship and mission. Baptist congregations today differ to some extent about the way that certain charismatic gifts are manifested and used but normally do not regard particular gifts such as speaking in tongues as a necessary evidence of conversion or baptism in the Spirit.

The Fellowship of Believers

Baptists understand that the church consists only of believers, those who have been born anew by God's Spirit and are committed in covenant to God and each other. This is a gathered church or believers' church, whose members have freely responded to the call of God to live and serve together. As the pioneer English Baptist Thomas Helwys declared in 1611, "the Church of Christ is a company of faithful people, separated from the world by the word and Spirit of God, being knit unto the Lord and unto one another, by baptism, upon their own confession of the faith and [confession of] sins" ("A Declaration of Faith of English People," art. 10).

Baptists, therefore, oppose the extreme individualism which regards the church as unnecessary. We become Christians personally, but when

What Baptists Believe

we belong to Christ, we belong to his body. The modern attempt to hold a private belief in Christ without belonging to a church is foreign to the New Testament. In the church we are bound together into a common vision and commitment, and this fellowship reflects and shares in the communion of God: Father, Son, and Holy Spirit.

Baptists hold that each local church has the freedom and the responsibility to conduct its own life and mission. The commitment flows from the belief that the risen Christ is fully present within the life of the gathered community (Matt. 18:20). A local church, gathered in what is often called "the church meeting," is responsible to discover the Lord's purposes for it. This involves questions about worship, mission, appointment of leaders, reception of members, and sharing of vision. Leaders will undoubtedly offer guidance, but in a Baptist church the congregation has the final authority, under Christ, for the life and mission of the church.

Sometimes tensions develop when individuals or a small group of leaders scheme to impose their ideas, but this is a distortion of the Baptist view, which insists that each believer should genuinely seek the common mind of Christ for the meeting. For the church meeting to work, there must be a shared commitment to know the mind of Christ as revealed through the Scriptures, prayer, and the wisdom of fellow believers.

At times this Baptist emphasis on the spiritual competency of the local church may have led to an exaggerated sense of autonomy and independence. This is one point on which Baptists around the world do evidence some differences. For some, the autonomy of the local church is absolute so that the role of any convention or union is minimal and only advisory, and it exists to facilitate ventures in which churches can achieve more together than separately. Other Baptists insist on the necessity of churches associating together; for them any definition of the church which does not include this interdependence is inadequate. According to this latter view, the local church needs to belong to a larger association of churches which can more fully reflect the nature of the church as it seeks to find the mind of Christ.

In any case, most Baptist churches show deep loyalties to sister churches, seek their advice and help, and cooperate in missions, education, and diakonal ministries. In such a cooperative spirit, Baptists are free to organize themselves in the way they believe will be most beneficial at any given time. For most Baptists, this sharing extends to fellowship in state and national Baptist conventions or unions and in the

WE BAPTISTS

BWA, and for some it also includes local ecumenical partnerships and membership in national and international councils of churches.

Baptists do not admit babies or very young children into church membership because they believe that baptism is intended only for repenting and confessing believers. Yet, they are not careless about children. They do not think that the salvation of anyone, including babies, is dependent upon baptism. They welcome children into the worshiping, instructional, and caring life of the church, often with a simple service of thanksgiving or dedication. They give themselves to guiding and teaching the gospel to children within their community with the hope and prayer that at a suitable time (nowhere officially defined by Baptists) they will come to personal faith, baptism, and responsible church membership.

Believer's Baptism by Immersion

Baptists affirm that baptism is for believers only. They judge that the New Testament teaches this. Moreover, they think that if the church should consist only of believers, then baptism as the way of initiation into the body of Christ should only be undertaken by responsible believers.

Baptists also hold that immersion, rather than sprinkling or pouring, is the appropriate mode for baptism. The mode seems to have been used in the New Testament and, more importantly, is consistent with the teaching on the believer's sharing in the death, burial, and resurrection of Christ in baptism (Rom. 6:3–4). The twentieth-century theologian Karl Barth, not a Baptist, once observed that primitive baptism had the character of a direct threat to life—if you stay under the water, you will drown—succeeded immediately by the corresponding deliverance and preservation, the raising from baptismal waters.

Baptist preachers and theologians have expended much effort to demonstrate the truth of these two points: baptism is by immersion and is only for believers. Baptism is important, however, not merely for our continuing identity as a denomination, but because it constantly calls us to the life of the disciple as we "put on Christ" in a visible and meaningful symbol.

The meaning of baptism is generally thought by Baptists to include the following:

1. It signifies the forgiveness of sin, both by the use of water, which washes the body, and by direct link with the death of Christ.

What Baptists Believe

2. It signifies death to the old life of sin and resurrection to the newness of life which comes through faith in Christ.

3. It signifies initiation into the visible membership of the church, the body of Christ.

4. It is confession by the believer of faith in Christ and of a desire to obey the Lord's every command.

5. It is a dramatic presentation of the basic gospel acts of our Lord's death and resurrection. As much as we sometimes have sanitized the rite with warm water, tiles, lights, and towels, immersion as an unlovely and humiliating act reminds us of the offense of the cross and of the way in which it runs counter to our natural desires.

6. It is linked in the Scriptures and in Christian experience with the gift of the Holy Spirit.

7. It symbolizes our belief in the power of God to raise us up at the final resurrection at the end of the age.

Baptism is both a human act (that is, of confession and dedication) and a moment for divine activity (that is, when God freely meets us anew with his gracious blessing). Both dimensions are involved, although Baptists differ on the emphasis they give to each aspect. Clearly, no person should be presented for baptism without there having been a prior activity of God. The baptismal candidate is there only because God has spoken to him or her and awakened faith in the heart.

Baptism is to be seen as one part of the total experience of conversion-baptism-church membership. The stages of this experience may be separated by a short or a long period of time. But in the total experience, three aspects are essential: the gracious activity of God, the response of faith, and then the profession of this faith. Certainly, baptism is not necessary for salvation; that takes place by grace alone through faith. But baptism in the New Testament is always the accompaniment of faith and is one part of that total experience which leads from the life of sin through the personal encounter with Christ into the fellowship of the church.

We Baptists

Church Membership

In New Testament days, baptism was closely connected with joining the Christian community. To be baptized and not to be a part of a local church was simply unthinkable. Today, some people are baptized who do not ever become members of any Christian church. Such a practice is contrary to New Testament teaching and Baptist principles. Indeed, many churches, having instructed the new believers, now incorporate into one act of worship the service of believer's baptism and the act of receiving the baptized into church membership at the Lord's table.

Most Baptist churches require that all those joining the church have been first baptized by immersion as believers. This is called close membership. Other Baptist churches recognize the sadness of the divisions in Christianity today and accept as members those who have been accepted as members of another church by another form of baptism. This might be baptism as a believer without immersion, or baptism as infants followed by public confession of faith at the time of confirmation. Some even receive members only on a verbal profession of faith without baptism. These are forms of open membership.

Whatever practical considerations are involved, however, Baptists believe that a return to the New Testament practice of baptism of believers by immersion is essential for a true understanding of the nature of faith, the church, and discipleship. The responsibilities of the church member include sharing in public worship, prayer, and church meetings and engaging in the evangelistic, educational, and caring life of the local church. Stewardship, which is the concept that all we are and have is a trust from God, leads the church member to support the local church's finances in a systematic manner. Fundamentally, of course, all members ought to serve God in their daily vocations and in the whole of their living.

The responsibility of members to each other was expressed in the first Baptist churches by the signing of a church covenant, through which members covenanted with God and with one another "to walk together in all his ways, known and to be made known to us." Even where formal signed covenants are not used today, the concept of a church as a covenant community remains in the practice of the congregation as members minister to one another throughout the journey of life.

The Priesthood of All Believers

The church is a fellowship of believers. Each member is in a personal relationship with the Head of the church. Accordingly, there are no

What Baptists Believe

degrees of status among Christians. Every Christian is called upon to fulfill the ministry of the church. Baptists have made much of the phrase, "the priesthood of all believers," although this has sometimes been misunderstood and misapplied.

Remarkably, from the Old Testament references to various aspects of priesthood, the only references taken up by New Testament writers and applied to the church are those in which the whole nation of Israel is described as a nation of priests (see Exod. 19:6; Isa. 61:6). In the New Testament the whole people of God comprise the priesthood; there are no priestly families or groups (see 1 Pet. 2:5, 9; Rev. 1:6; 5:10; 20:6). As a priesthood the church exercises two basic functions: it goes to God on behalf of humankind, and to humankind on behalf of God. It has a worshiping and witnessing function. The BWA statement on Baptist identity (1989) noted: "Baptists have always been a praying people, in both corporate prayer and in encouraging a pattern of individual spirituality that requires each member to engage in regular prayer and Bible study."

The priesthood of all believers includes also what might be called "the prophethood of all believers." To share in the telling forth or proclamation of the gospel is a necessary function of priesthood (1 Pet. 2:9). All believers are to be involved, therefore, in this worshiping and witnessing life of the church.

The Ministry

Every Christian is in the ministry of the church. When someone becomes a Christian and joins the local church, he or she becomes a minister or servant of God. There are no laity and clergy in the popular use of those terms. The church is people, and the church as a whole is the minister of God. Wherever the people go, there the church goes.

But to say that all are equal in the life of the church or that all church members are ministers of the gospel does not mean that all members have the same function within the church. The early Baptists insisted that a local church was only a complete church when it had appointed its necessary spiritual leaders. These were the pastor, sometimes known as the elder or the bishop, and deacons. Specialized ministers are gifts from the ascended Christ to his church (Eph. 4:11–13). In order to emphasize this truth, early Baptists ordained both pastors and deacons. Ordination gave evidence that these people were set apart for special tasks. No one was ordained hastily. The church solemnly expressed its conviction in an outward way that these persons had received a prior inward call from God.

WE BAPTISTS

Today, Baptist churches still set aside both pastors and deacons for particular service, although these offices might be called by a variety of terms. In some large urban congregations, others are associated with the pastor in his ministry. Some churches also appoint elders to assist the pastor. Many churches refer to the setting aside of deacons and elders as ordination, although they would understand this action as having a different purpose from the ordination of pastors. In most Baptist churches today, deacons assist in the spiritual leadership of the church as well as care for material aspects of the church's life.

The great majority of Baptist churches call men to be their pastors. Some congregations today recognize the call of both men and women to the pastorate. Likewise, Baptist congregations differ in whether only men or both women and men should serve as deacons. These differences reflect various interpretations of the Scriptures. Pastors are recognized as preachers of the Word of God and leaders of the congregation in its worship. Most churches ordain pastors by the laying on of hands. In some conventions and unions, this occurs only after theological education has been completed. Although a local church is always free to call any person to serve as a pastor, some Baptist bodies will only accredit those ministers whose calling and gifts have been recognized by a wider representative body of churches.

The pastor exercises a spiritual leadership, that of a servant to the church, and seeks to help the congregation to find and exercise the variety of gifts found in the life of the church. To build up the local fellowship in knowledge and caring is a major task of a Baptist pastor. It is not that the pastor is to be the sole evangelistic agent, but rather that church members continuously function in the world while the pastor seeks to equip them for their work and witness (Eph. 4:12).

The Lord's Supper

An important feature of Christian worship is the Lord's Supper, or Communion. Some few Baptists, reckoning the Lord's Supper as an integral part of the normal pattern of worship, observe the Lord's Supper every Sunday. Others observe the Supper twice a month, once a month, or once a quarter. Most are convinced that, whenever the meal takes place, it should be observed on a regular basis and be regarded as a vital component of the total act of worship.

Baptists observe the Lord's Supper congregationally; that is, deacons have a part in distributing the elements, which are often then handed from one member of the congregation to another. As each member passes

What Baptists Believe

the bread or cup to a fellow member, he or she is reminded that the Lord's Supper is a community meal of the family of God and a corporate act of the church. It is not intended to be a private communion. Only believers are able to share meaningfully in the Lord's Supper. Some Baptist churches gladly welcome Christians from other denominations to partake of the elements in the Supper (open communion). Other Baptist churches restrict such partaking to those who have received believer's baptism by immersion or even to the members of the church observing the Supper (close communion).

The meaning of the Lord's Supper is derived from the New Testament. It is an act of remembrance, for the breaking of the bread and pouring of the cup assist Christians in recalling the significance of Christ's death. It is an act of communion, for they meet in the living presence of the Christ who commanded them to do this and who unites his people. It is an act of thanksgiving, as they recall all that his death and continued presence mean. It is an act of hope, as they continue this celebration "until he comes."

Baptists believe that, since Christ is truly present with his people, he ministers to them in a special way at the communion service. But they have been hesitant to define more precisely the blessing of the memorial Supper. The blessing is not automatic and not confined in some physical sense to the elements. Yet, the obedient, humble, and expectant Christian is blessed by meeting Christ and his people at the Lord's table.

Religious Freedom

The passion of Baptists for complete religious freedom is central to their identity. John Smyth's followers declared:

> That the magistrate is not by virtue of his office to meddle with religion, or matters of conscience, to force and compel men to this or that form of religion, or doctrine: but to leave Christian religion free, to every man's conscience, and to handle only civil transgressions (Rom. 13), injuries and wrongs of man against man, in murder, adultery, theft, etc., for Christ only is the king, and lawgiver of the church and conscience (James 4:12)—"Propositions and Conclusions," art. 84.

Thomas Helwys, Roger Williams, Isaac Backus, John Leland, J. G. Oncken, William Knibb, Paul Besson, and other Baptists have advocated religious freedom. On the basis of the sovereignty of God, which no human being can assume, Baptists have always pleaded for full religious

31

WE BAPTISTS

freedom not only for themselves but for others, whatever their religion. The principle of religious liberty is indeed the cornerstone of all human rights. British Baptists have resisted any governmental infringement on the "Crown Rights of the Redeemer."

The 1963 Baptist Faith and Message Statement, article 17, of the Southern Baptist Convention proclaimed:

> God alone is Lord of the conscience, and He has left it free from the doctrines and commandments of men which are contrary to His Word or not contained in it. Church and state should be separate. The state owes to every church protection and full freedom in the pursuit of its spiritual ends. In providing for such freedom no ecclesiastical group or denomination should be favored by the state more than others. . . . A free church in a free state is the Christian ideal. . . .

But religious freedom must be differentiated from other freedoms. Religious freedom is a civil freedom, a freedom from any compulsion and coercion by the state or national church in matters of religious faith and practice. Quite distinct is the Christian freedom which results from the saving work of Christ. Yet the latter should not be taken to mean that any individual is free to believe and act in complete disregard of Christian orthodoxy and standards of morality. True Christian freedom must be coupled with responsibility. Church discipline was a strong feature of early Baptist life. At the same time, Baptists affirm the need to preserve freedom of conscience and therefore accept some differences among Baptists.

THE MISSION OF CHRIST TO THE NATIONS

We now return to where we started with an emphasis on the kingdom of God. Baptists believe that every Christian and every church have the serious obligation to obey the Great Commission of Jesus Christ (Matt. 28:18–20 and parallels) by seeking to make disciples of all human beings and to teach all that Jesus has commanded. Personal evangelism should be one of the great passions of Baptist people. The planting of Christian congregations among all the people groups of the world is a goal of evangelization. Working for justice, reconciliation, and peace is an essential part of the mission of Baptists.

What Baptists Believe

At the advent of the twenty-first century, Baptists are linked with all Christians who would likewise labor for the fulfillment of the Great Commission, being mindful of Jesus' saying: "And this gospel of the kingdom will be preached in the whole world as a testimony to all nations, and then the end will come" (Matt. 24:14). Together, as we labor in the power of the Holy Spirit, we long for the second appearing of our Lord Jesus Christ, the resurrection of the dead, the consummation of all things, and the eternal kingdom of God.

CHAPTER THREE

How Baptists Make Moral Decisions

WHEN THE BAPTIST WORLD ALLIANCE (BWA) WAS FORMED IN 1905, the president called on all those present to stand and, as their very first act together, to recite the Apostles' Creed. On the face of it, this act was a very unusual thing to do because Baptists do not use creeds as many other Christians do. The president was calling the representatives in this act to affirm and demonstrate that Baptists belong in the continuity of the historic Church.

In other words, Baptists are not some off-beat sect with their own self-created ideas about God. We are orthodox Christians. Even though we Baptists have distinctive insights into the gospel and the life in Christ, we stand in the great tradition of the Christian Church built on the one foundation (1 Cor. 3:11; Eph. 2:20), believing and proclaiming the faith once delivered to the saints (Jude 3).

BEGINNING WITH GOD

Hence, Baptists believe in God, Maker of heaven and earth (Gen. 1). We believe in God the Creator of all human beings, men and women, made in the image of God and answerable to God (Gen. 1:27). We believe that God has a will and way for human beings to obey and that in that will are our peace and freedom. Out of love for us, God gives humankind instructions and with them the freedom to obey or disobey (Deut. 30:15–20).

34

How Baptists Make Moral Decisions

Such freedom and responsibility are real because, in fact, part of our sad human story includes an unwillingness to trust God, so that in unbelief we disobey God's laws and fall from God's high calling. This disobedience is real, and it has serious consequences. It underlines the fact that we are beings with moral power and choice, for good and for evil. Yet, our life is before God. When we understand ourselves aright, we know we are dependent creatures, stewards and not owners, answerable and accountable to God. To believe and act otherwise is to sin, and that is a much more serious state in which to be than people often recognize.

To illustrate, sometimes we speak and act as if the creation is ours to do with as we will. In this arrogance we pollute and destroy what God has given, only to bring further destruction on ourselves. Baptists see the ecological threat as having its roots in a neglect of the truth of God. Our sin is serious. Our children and children's children will know the consequences.

But we also believe in God our Savior. We believe that God loved the world so much that he sent his only Son to live and die to save us from the consequences of our sinful disobedience (John 3:16). Jesus is the Son of God, the full expression of the love which God has for us and of his desire to save us (Rom. 5:6–11; 2 Cor. 5:19). Jesus came proclaiming God's kingdom, calling people to repent and believe the good news (Mark 1:15). In his ministry of teaching, healing, and exorcising, he showed the power, love, desire, and will of God (Luke 4:18–19). He challenged the sinful choices people made and the erroneous understandings they had about the will of God. This brought him enemies, and such is the extent of human freedom and sin that they conspired against him and killed him. Yet it was not so much that people took his life as that he gave it in sacrificial love (John 10:18). The cross of Jesus becomes the place where all the sin and disobedience of the world come to focus and where the eternal love and will of God to save find fullest expression. What was the outcome?

Easter morning followed! God raised Jesus from the dead. That was a victory over death itself and over all that death represents, all the sin that culminates in our death and separation from God by our own choice. Yet, God remains God and has the last and final word. The resurrection of Jesus means that everything has to be looked at in a new light, God's light. The cycle of sin has been broken by God. It means beyond all doubt that Jesus is the one to be utterly obeyed. He is the one to whom all authority in heaven and on earth has been given (Matt. 28:18). He is Lord

(Acts 2:36)! The last and final word in all human affairs is Jesus Christ, living word, Son of God, Savior. In the last analysis, he is the one to be honored, praised, and obeyed (Phil. 2:9–11; Rev. 21:6).

Baptists, together with other Christians, acknowledge the authority of Jesus Christ. At the heart of our baptism is the confession, "Jesus Christ is Lord!" But we come to this confession, we believe, by the work of the Holy Spirit. We believe that the Holy Spirit is God in action, creating, saving, healing, and renewing. The Holy Spirit opens our eyes to the truth and reality of God. The Spirit takes the things of Christ and shows them to us (John 14:26; 15:26; 16:13–14). Without this work of the Holy Spirit, there is no knowledge of God for us, no awareness of the truth of our salvation, and no guidance in the way and will of God. So we must be born of water and the Spirit, born again, born from above, born of God (John 3:5–7; Rom. 8:12–17). God graciously gives us faith, and so, by the work of God, we who once were lost and in darkness have been found and restored and set again on our feet to walk in the ways of God.

GRACE AND WORKS

We Baptists follow the biblical pattern when we begin reflections on how we make moral decisions by recalling first the nature of God in Trinity: Father, Son, and Holy Spirit—God our Creator, Savior, and Sanctifier. To say this is to do more than make an orthodox confession of faith or repeat sound doctrine. In our baptism we are baptized into the name of God: Father, Son, and Holy Spirit (Matt. 28:19). That implies that we are baptized into the life of God and into the mission of God. The life we now live is not to be reduced to formal self-generated obedience to rules or the intellectual affirmation of right doctrine. It is more dynamic than that. It is life in God lived by grace through faith. It is life in fellowship with God in the living, new being of God's creation. It is life in and by the power of the triune God.

Thus, Baptists do not see the moral life as a matter of making ourselves moral by obeying the law. Paul the apostle knew that that was an impossibility, and he had tried harder than most (Rom. 7:21–24; Phil. 3:2–11). Because God is God in Trinity, the kind of God whose life finds expression only in this mutuality of life-giving love, then to be baptized into the name of the Trinity means that we live in God and God in us. It means that the life we now live we live by faith in the Son of God who loved us and gave himself for us (Gal. 2:20). The Christian life is not a moral achievement but

How Baptists Make Moral Decisions

a gift of grace with the resources to fulfill the laws of God. So God can achieve in us, and even through us, what we could never do for ourselves. This is why, in all our weakness, Baptists praise God because we know that we are saved from the consequences of our sin and from the impossibility of moral achievements in order that God, by his power, might do more abundantly than all we can ever ask or imagine (Eph. 3:20–21).

Baptists, following the New Testament, believe that being a Christian is not a matter first of being moral but of being saved. From first to last, it is the work of God. Our ethical reflections are grounded in the grace of our Lord Jesus Christ, the love of God, and the fellowship of the Holy Spirit (2 Cor. 13:14).

God saves and renews us by grace and not because of our works lest anyone should boast that she or he is a moral person (Eph. 2:8–9). Grace and law, however, are not to be separated. The Christian realizes this and, unlike the unspiritual person who is intent on personal interests, knows that God gives his law as a work of grace. We are not left in darkness. We have the Word of God, which is a lamp to our feet and a light to our path (Ps. 119:105), and our delight is in doing God's work and law (Ps. 119:97). We do it no longer as a curse or as a means to justify ourselves but out of gladness and gratitude, because in God's will is our peace and in his service is perfect freedom. Ethical obedience flows from grace. It is the service which the free person in Christ delights to give.

An important difference between being a person and a thing is that each person has his/her own will. We are rightly dismayed when persons are dealt with impersonally, taken for granted, pushed around, and exploited by others, for then they are not treated as the persons they are before God. God treats us as persons; consequently, we have our own wills. This is a matter of privilege and responsibility.

Baptists hold that, although many circumstances may affect and even constrain us, we are responsible to God for the choices we make and the actions we take. This view of what it is to be human arises from our understanding of God in Trinity. It means that we are moral beings with freedom because God made us so. He seeks not to compel us but for us to share freely with him the life to which he calls us.

FREEDOM, CHOICE, AND RESPONSIBILITY

God also calls us to bear the responsibility of decision-making. If we were robots, God could program us. If we were to be treated as those who

WE BAPTISTS

have no will to be respected and acknowledged so that we should only follow orders, then presumably, like a dictator, God would impose his will and allow no other. But God calls us by grace to discipleship of our own free will. When the crowds started to leave, Jesus asked his disciples if they really wanted to stay with him. They had a choice (John 6:67). This choice is reflected in our understanding and practice of baptism. No one can be forced into baptism. Being in Christ involves both God's gracious call and our free response. At baptism each candidate is asked whether he/she personally acknowledges the love of God, repents of sin, receives the salvation offered in Jesus Christ, and promises to live in obedience to the Lord in the fellowship of the church. No one can say and do this for another.

God gives us both the privilege and the responsibility of choice. We might at times wish that everything were clear and unambiguous and that we were told exactly what to do in every situation. But God is not like that. He has made us as persons and seeks us in personal relationship. As such, we are given freedom and responsibility to choose.

So how shall we choose rightly? This is always a pressing question for those who are serious about discipleship. Let us acknowledge that Baptists, and indeed other Christians, have not always agreed upon some very significant moral decisions. For example, there have always been some Christians who have found it morally impossible, as Christians, to go to war and kill other people. Other Christians, for the most part, have reluctantly disagreed with them and have fought and killed. Examples could quickly be given of other disagreements within Christ's church. All Christians have, in the Holy Spirit, an infallible guide to truth. But the fact is that we are not yet wholly free from sin; hence, none of us has an infallible apprehension of the Spirit's guidance. We can be wrong, and sometimes the church has had to acknowledge that fact; for example, the church came to see that it was wrong to think that a Spirit-led interpretation of the Bible could condone slavery.

This thought does not lead Baptists to a fearful paralysis of inaction for two important reasons. First, even if we do make a mistake, an erroneous judgment, that is not the end of the matter, because where we have acted in sincerity, God has promised to forgive us and is able to bring new beginnings from the disasters of our life. God is the God of resurrection, who can make all things new, lift up the fallen, and restore the sinner. So although we should not be arrogant and irresponsible about our actions, neither should we be afraid of error because the last word is with God.

How Baptists Make Moral Decisions

The prodigal son is not told to live crushed with his self-inflicted disaster. He is welcomed back to a new life (Luke 15:11–24). Peter, who denied his Lord at the first challenge to his loyalty, is nevertheless entrusted with the care of God's people (John 21:15–19). Such is the promise of the gospel. It gives us courage to make the decisions we must make, even if we are not always certain of all that we are doing.

A second reason why we should have a modest confidence in our moral decision-making is that God has given and gives us guidance in vitally important ways. Baptists go about making moral decisions by following these ways. Let us take them one by one.

JESUS IS LORD IN THE COMMUNITY OF FAITH

First, our confession that Jesus Christ is Lord is central and crucial. He is the one to whom all final and absolute authority has been given (Matt. 28:18). So, in the simplest of terms, Christian ethics is about doing and living as Jesus Christ would want. If anyone should suggest a way of behavior which is clearly contradictory of the teaching and life of Jesus, then Baptists would say that that is no way to live. Such behavior would be wrong in Christian eyes because Jesus Christ is Lord. We take such affirmation to have massive moral consequences in the lives of disciples and, we might add, also for the world.

On many moral matters that confront us as dilemmas today, the gospel records of Jesus have no direct teaching to give us. For example, nowhere in the Gospels can one find any specific teaching from Jesus on whether we should build more nuclear power stations. This does not compromise the significance of Jesus. Remember, we have already acknowledged that God requires that we take the burden of decision. What is important is that the church goes on telling and listening to the story of Jesus so that it becomes deep within us, shaping our responses and guiding our thoughts. It is one way by which, in the Spirit, Jesus lives in us. The church, by constantly telling and reflecting on the story of Jesus, becomes a community of Christian character, not by human achievement but by grace. Remembering God's grace is essential if we are to make Christian moral decisions.

This emphasis on the corporate life of the church is important. We shall take up one vital aspect of it with regard to decision-making later, but, for the moment, we reflect on how our characters are shaped and

WE BAPTISTS

how we become moral persons. We have learned much of what we come to practice in our behavior from those who initially cared for us and from the overall context in which they gave that care. The values we affirm and the character we develop owe a great deal to the communities which nurtured us and the teaching they gave us.

Such communities vary widely. Thus, the child of grasping, greedy, quarreling, loveless parents receives one picture of human relationships and personal goals for human life. This is bound to be different from the situation of a child in a home where mutual love, care, service, and the seeking of the welfare of others are predominant and God is honored.

Families and larger communities, like congregations, are shaped by their memories. They tell stories and remember significant events, events that might not even have been noticed by others. But these stories make and keep the community what it is. If the story should be forgotten, then identity is lost, and something else forms character.

Baptists gather, or are gathered by God, in congregations each Sunday to hear again the story. We are gathered around the Bible and listen carefully as it is read. We think, talk, and pray together about how we are to live as God's people or how we are to be genuinely a biblical people. We ask forgiveness for our sins and claim the promises of God. We come to the Lord's Table and with bread and wine remember the saving love of Jesus Christ our Lord. True, we read the Bible personally and seek to obey its message in our individual lives, but our belonging together in the church of Christ is the context in which Christian character goes on being shaped and developed.

For this reason, we are careful to tell our children the story of Jesus so that they should be shaped in the community that tries to live out the life in Christ. Later, the child will grow to make his/her own decision to be a disciple, but, because we love our children, we tell them the story of God's ways in the context of Christian love and nurture. Christian character is shaped in the context of the church. It is a matter of growth for young and old, to be completed only in heaven (Phil. 3:12–14).

GOD'S WORD WRITTEN

But who is Jesus Christ? We must admit that all sorts of people, including Baptists, have at times made Christ after their own image. They have used their Jesus to support a decision which they have already made on other grounds. How do we prevent that distortion from

How Baptists Make Moral Decisions

happening? By stressing, as Baptists do, the authority of the Bible. Jesus who is Lord is not the Jesus I make for myself but the one to whom the Holy Scriptures bear witness. Here is the fundamental record of the incarnate Word. Hence, the Bible is essential for Baptists in making moral decisions. Whatever post-biblical Christians have said, or are saying, about any particular issue, the ultimate test to which we would bring ourselves and everyone else is Scripture. The Bible is the written Word that bears testimony to Jesus Christ the incarnate Word.

Of course, Baptists argue about the correct interpretation of Scripture and the exact nature of its authority, but all Baptists recognize that the Bible is authoritative. Here is the record of God's ways with us, and we continually turn to the Bible for the guidance of God, in the expectation that "the Lord had more truth and light yet to break forth out of his Holy Word" (John Robinson, "Parting Advice").

We do recognize that Christians interpret the Bible differently. We must not avoid that fact, but neither must we allow it to qualify out of existence our appeal to the Scriptures. There is an important distinction between the authority of the Bible and the authority of my interpretation of the Bible. Sometimes, people have tried to say that their interpretation is the only valid one, and they may be right, but since we are not God, and ultimate authority lies with Christ, no one should try to force or claim an authority for one's own view.

Baptists believe that the Scriptures were inspired by God and that God the Holy Spirit is the Bible's best interpreter. The fact that none of us can claim an infallible apprehension of the Spirit's guidance should not make us lose confidence in the fact that the Spirit does guide us. The experience of Christians reveals that the Spirit calls to our minds words of the Bible that give us comfort and guidance and also rebuke us. We believe in a living God who is neither deaf to our prayers nor dumb before our need of his word. Believing, as Baptists do, in the Trinitarian being of God, we rejoice in the work of the Spirit to open blind eyes and deaf ears (John 16:13–14). "The Spirit breathes upon the word, and brings the truth to sight" (William Cowper's hymn). That should give us further courage as, in the process of moral decision-making, we listen to the Scriptures and pray for God to guide us.

The seeking of God and his will in prayer cannot be overemphasized. Since we are seeking together the mind of the Lord and yet recognize our own sinfulness and inability to discern the truth, we call on God as children might ask of a father (Matt. 7:7–11). Prayer is not simply a factor in an ethical method. It is the air we breathe in the fellowship of the Holy Spirit.

41

We Baptists

THE FELLOWSHIP OF BELIEVERS

Many references to the Holy Spirit in the New Testament make it clear that the Spirit is given to and is at work in the church as much as in individual lives. Here we pick up again the question about the interpretation of the Scriptures. Baptists have as their most distinctive doctrine the doctrine of the church. We believe in the gathered church, or the fellowship of believers. We are not a gathering of the like-minded but of those called by God and held together in his covenant love. In this God-given fellowship, the church listens to the Scriptures, prays and shares together, and tries to discern together the leading of the Holy Spirit.

Baptists do not believe in a hierarchy of authority, as if some people by reason of their office can tell the church what to do. In experience, we may come to realize that some in the fellowship are given gifts of wisdom and insight, and thus we listen particularly carefully to them. But we all—pastor, preacher, elder, deacon, member—submit to one another in the fellowship of the gospel, living as those who submit ultimately only to Jesus. We test our judgments in the meeting of the church gathered under the Word of God.

Baptists affirm the gospel competency of every local congregation gathered in the name and under the authority of Christ. We believe that no one can or should compel any congregation to act and understand the faith in ways that its members have not themselves agreed before God. Hence, each congregation is required to seek the mind of Christ and has the responsibility to interpret and actualize Christ's purposes. The theological ground of this conviction is that Jesus Christ is the one to whom all authority has been given. Since Christ is the head of the church, then the members must together seek his will. But with the living Christ as Lord present among them as they meet in his name, they are subject to no other authorities.

A wise congregation, however, will seek the help of others or heed any resolutions or affirmations made by local associations, unions, conventions, or Baptists gathered together in the BWA. None of these has power over the local congregation gathered in the name of Jesus, but any such congregation will want to hear what other Christians, and especially fellow Baptists, are saying as they come themselves to seek the mind of the Lord on difficult issues.

Disagreement may arise within a congregation on a moral issue. What then? In the end, the congregation will have to decide. Some Baptists have lived for a long time, for example, with a division of opinion on

How Baptists Make Moral Decisions

issues of peace and justice. Both sides of the argument appeal to the Scriptures and eventually agree to allow the disagreement to stand as a matter of conscience. But it becomes a different matter when some are convinced that one way of behavior is a contradiction of the gospel of Christ and his laws. If that should become the mind of the church, then it becomes a matter of discipline. Paul was very straight with a congregation in Corinth that was prepared to tolerate immorality in its membership (1 Cor. 5). Yet, discipline must also reflect the mind of Christ and his pastoral heart toward the wayward.

We have identified three crucial factors which shape how Baptists make moral judgments: the Lordship of Jesus Christ, the authority of the Scriptures, and the fellowship of believers, which is the church. In simple terms, making moral judgments involves asking:

> *What would Jesus Christ do?*
> *What does the Bible teach?*
> *What do we together think is the mind of Christ as taught by the Spirit?*

Where these questions are asked in the openness of faith and trust by those earnestly seeking to know God's will, there, we believe, God is at work to guide his people by the Spirit. There are no guarantees that we will always get the right answers and do the right deeds, but at least we are trying to be alert to God and desiring to live out his call in faithfulness.

FACTS, WISDOM, MOTIVES, CONSEQUENCES, AND DUTY

Is there anything else that needs to be kept in mind? Yes. We cannot make a sensible judgment on some moral issues without knowing the basic facts of the matter. These are often complex and call for an expert's attention. Sometimes such experts are members of our churches, and so the congregation ought to listen to their contribution on the basis of the knowledge they have. Judging in willful ignorance of the facts does nothing to honor the Lord of glory.

Then, also, churches ought to pay attention to what might be called secular wisdom. The church may simply judge that wisdom to be wrong because it conflicts in a direct way with the teaching of Christ through Scripture. None of us should be unduly impressed by the "wisdom belonging to this passing age" (1 Cor. 2:6, NEB), but neither should we ignore the fact that God has not left himself without witnesses and sometimes has spoken through others to his people. So, we listen to contemporary wisdom but bring it all to the test of Christ in Scripture.

Again, the church might ask itself some questions that have often been part of moral inquiries. For example, what motives are at work here? We recognize, as the sinners we are, that motives are never entirely pure. Some serious introspective reflection might alert us to issues which we have overlooked, or been tempted to ignore, or have misrepresented by reason of our self-interest.

We also might ask about the consequences of taking a given action. What will follow if we do this? The trouble is that consequences can be unpredictable and hard to determine, whether they are short-term or long-term.

Or, we might ask about any sense of duty which goes with the moral action we are contemplating. Do we think it right in itself, because it has its own inner authority, or do we only think it is right because other persons who seem to have a particular authority say so? That is, is there a sense that we ought to do it because we can do no other?

These are classical ways by which people have thought about moral decisions. Baptists, along with all those who recognize that we live in a moral universe, take these questions into account, but at the heart of the matter is our desire to be true to God's call and word as revealed in Jesus Christ.

A TEST CASE FROM HISTORY

How does all this work out in practice? Let us take an issue on which Baptists have taken a stand of some consequence: religious freedom for all. The first publicly to defend this position in print was Thomas Helwys, leader of the first Baptist church on English soil. He argued, against the prevailing assumptions of the power of monarchs and other rulers, that whereas in matters of earthly obedience in the life of the state the rulers had every right to claim and expect our obedience, in any matters of faith, those fundamental questions between God and the believer, the king had no authority. Helwys argued:

> for men's religion to God, is betwixt God and themselves; the King shall not answer for it, neither may the King be judge between God and man. Let them be heretics, Turks, Jews, or whatsoever it appertains not to the

How Baptists Make Moral Decisions

earthly power to punish them in the least measure. This is made evident to our lord the King by the scriptures (*The Mistery of Iniquity,* 1612, p. 69).

It is wrong to try to compel belief. It is wrong to refuse someone freedom of conscience to believe what he will. Helwys was challenging the absolute right of any human authority. Many saw his position as being politically dangerous, even subversive, as indeed it is in any totalitarian state. But notice how Helwys defended his argument. He appealed to the Bible. No king could claim authority over the conscience of another human being. That authority belonged to Jesus Christ alone. So today, Baptists argue for religious freedom for all, and the ground of that argument is not in the first place an appeal to human rights but to divine sovereignty. The sovereignty of God guarantees the freedom of humankind.

BAPTISTS AND ETHICAL ISSUES TODAY

The BWA has a Christian Ethics Commission. At its regular meetings, the range of issues raised by the worldwide Baptist family is enormous, predictably so from a people who want to share God's mission in the world. So, at recent meetings, for example, deep concern about the nature and shape of family life came out of Africa. Social changes in the culture, the fearsome spread of AIDS, economic poverty, and wretched tribal warfare were identified as being crucial matters which claim the attention of Baptists in their calling to be faithful to the triune God.

Concerns about the social effects of urbanization and the unequal distribution of fundamental resources come from Latin America. Issues of lifestyle, both individual and corporate, challenge the Christian church. With other Christians, Baptists have had to face the fact that in some situations particular choices have to be made, priorities adopted, and preferential options taken up.

At one commission meeting, a North American pastor called for the importance of ethical reflection not simply in our seminaries but as a regular feature in the life of local churches. The speed of change and the way in which ethical decision-making is more likely to be reactive than preemptive were seen as features of the context in which Baptists found themselves. The issue of racism was recognized as one that still had to be thoroughly faced.

We Baptists

European Baptists recognize that Baptists on their continent face the rise of nationalistic and ethnic identities, which have both positive and negative consequences. What does it mean for us to be both loyal to Christ and to Spain or Germany or any other nation? Moreover, Europe, as the homeland of the Enlightenment, has to face fundamental questions about truth and knowledge and where wisdom is to be found.

One factor is true for us all: the recognition that many of our descriptions of moral behavior relate to our own context. Thus, for example, some Baptists who know the difficulty which goes with being a small minority group in a secular country might well emphasize, as of deep importance, an issue which Baptists in another context might not be so troubled about at all. Behind this choice might be a strong missiological emphasis, a way of keeping and developing the witness of those called to live the life in Christ. Baptists have been known to divide over such issues as dancing. Here we ought to pay attention to Paul's teaching about not dividing the church by giving needless offense but respecting one another's consciences (1 Cor. 8:7–13).

All of these and many more issues come before Baptists. Increasingly, Baptists are finding the challenge to Christian discipleship a severe one in maintaining the practical witness of Christian living. Both in local church groups and in regional and national bodies, we are giving time and careful attention to working out the way of Christian obedience. We want to remain true to the Scriptures as followers of the Lord Jesus Christ. We believe that the Holy Spirit will be the guide of those who openly seek the guidance of God. We are grateful for the contribution which we make to one another as we share reflections and resources. We honor those who speak and live boldly in the name of Jesus, offering a prophetic witness to the world. Finally, we are grateful that through our national unions and conventions, and especially through the BWA, we are able to address governments and call them to honor the ways and will of God.

Peter, in his first letter, quotes an important word which God spoke to his ancient people. The apostle is writing to congregations that are finding the life of discipleship challenging and at times a little unnerving in the light of the attitudes of their contemporaries. The word is, "'You shall be holy, for I am holy'" (Lev. 11:44–45; 19:2; 1 Pet. 1:16, RSV). God's holiness is more than his moral perfection, just as our call to holiness is more than to ethical goodness. For us to be holy means that all our living belongs to God and that we are to live in the conviction that we realize

How Baptists Make Moral Decisions

the truth of our baptism, that we are called to share the life of God, right now as well as in glory. The challenge of Christian ethics is therefore not something additional to the gospel, a kind of add-on optional extra for the few. The call to holiness, to faithful discipleship in following Jesus, is part of the privilege of the people of God, who know that they are created, redeemed, and guided by the living God—Father, Son, and Holy Spirit—to whom be praise, honor, and glory, forever.

CHAPTER FOUR

Baptists in Worship

THE CHRISTIAN CHURCH WAS BORN IN WORSHIP. "THEY devoted themselves to the apostles' teaching and to the fellowship, to the breaking of bread and to prayer. Everyone was filled with awe. . . . Every day they continued to meet together . . . and ate with glad and sincere hearts, praising God" (Acts 2:42–43, 46–47, NIV). Writing some years after Pentecost, Paul could actually define Christians by their worship: "We" are those "who worship by the Spirit of God, who glory in Christ Jesus, and put no confidence in the flesh" (Phil.3:3). It comes as no surprise, accordingly, that the consummation of the Christian pilgrimage is expressed as a worshiping community: "There before me was a great multitude . . . from every nation, tribe, people and language, standing . . . in front of the Lamb. . . . They cried out: 'Salvation belongs to our God, who sits on the throne, and to the Lamb'" (Rev. 7:9–10). In common with all other Christians, Baptists are a worshiping people, defined and shaped to a significant degree by their experiences in worship.

Our history reflects how worship has helped to shape Baptists. The earliest recognizably Baptist congregation, John Smyth's church in Amsterdam in 1609, is identified in terms of its worship services—two per Sunday, each approaching four hours' duration, and consisting primarily of the reading and prophetic exposition of Scripture. The Second London Baptist Confession of Faith of 1689 states that "the Lord Jesus calleth . . . those that are given unto him by his Father . . . to walk together in particular societies, or Churches, for their mutual

Baptists in Worship

edification; and the due performance of that public worship, which he requireth of them in the World" (ch. 26, sect. 5).

As we enter a new millennium, the picture is unchanged. In all parts of the globe, being a Baptist believer carries at its heart a commitment to the worship services of a local Baptist congregation. During the last thirty years, throughout worldwide Christianity, worship has become a focus of attention and debate, more so than at anytime since the Protestant Reformation.

WHY WE WORSHIP

The first and best reason for worship is simply that God is who he is! By his very nature, God is infinitely and eternally worthy of worship. Karl Barth argued that the word "God" is a vocative term. That means we only use "God" correctly when we implicitly say, "O God!" and in our hearts bow to him in adoring worship. In the final analysis, we worship because we have no choice. To fail to worship would be to deny God's existence as the living God. Thus, in thinking and speaking about God right now as we read this chapter, we are drawn into worship! For we are not thinking and speaking about some god-being, somewhere out there. Rather, we are relating to the ever-blessed God, who is present at this moment and is utterly worthy of our adoration and praise. When we refer to God, we are not speaking about who he is, but about who you are! We are already worshiping.

In exploring worship, a helpful starting point is the conversation recorded in Acts 22 between the glorified Jesus and Saul of Tarsus. Saul asked two questions, "'Who are you, Lord?'" and "'What shall I do, Lord?'" (Acts 22:8, 10). The order of these questions is crucial. The "Who?" question came first, "'Who are you, Lord?'" The answer to that question, "'I am Jesus . . . ,'" shaped the answer to Saul's subsequent "What?" question: "'What shall I do, Lord?'" In our thinking about worship, we need, like Paul, to begin with the "Who?" and ask "Who are you, Lord?" As God answers that question by revealing himself to us, we are in a position to ask and have answered our further question, "What do you want us to do when we worship?"

Who is God? Over the centuries Baptists, along with all other Christians, have listened to God's witness to himself in the Bible. As a result, they have spoken of God using three words: Father, Son, and Spirit (Matt. 28:19; 2 Cor. 13:14). Each of these words and all three together answer the question why Baptists and all other Christians worship.

49

WE BAPTISTS

First, God is Father. This title arises within the being of God himself; supremely, the Father is the "Father of our Lord Jesus Christ" (1 Pet. 1:3). John Calvin referred to him as the "fount of Deity," from whom the Son and Spirit eternally come forth. Today's deeply felt concerns over gender-biased language and the human tragedy of failed fatherhood notwithstanding, he is also, according to Jesus, "Our Father" (Matt. 6:9). As such, he is the source and origin of our existence, our creator, and life-sustainer, infinitely exalted over all things, the God "from whom and through whom and to whom are all things" (Rom. 11:36). Here is over-whelming reason for worship. Our lives and the entire life of the created universe are derived from him and are sustained every moment by his upholding power. He rules over all things in the universe in the fulfillment of his glorious purposes. With the men and women of Scripture, we fall before our Creator-Father in awe-filled worship (Exod. 3:4–6; Ps. 139; 150; Isa. 6:1–5; 40:12–31; Rev. 4:1–11).

Second, God is Son. Without ceasing for a moment to be all that is implied in being "Father," he is God a second time as God the Son. There is a richness of life in God by which he exists in a community of persons. Love and relationship belong to his essence. In the miracle of his grace, this second person entered our space and time as Jesus Christ (John 1:14; Matt. 1:18; Luke 1:35; Gal. 4:4).

The Bible sets this entry of God into our human life in the context of our sin and wretchedness (Matt. 1:21; Luke 2:11; 19:9–10; John 1:29; Gal. 4:4). He came to reveal the Father (Matt. 11:27; John 1:18; 14:9). But he did that in the context of reconciling us to the Father by his self-sacrifice on the cross and in glorious resurrection (Heb. 2:14; 1 John 4:10; Rom. 4:25; 1 Cor. 15:3–4).

Here are further, even profounder, reasons for our worship. No wonder Christians "glory in Christ Jesus" (Phil. 3:3)! That God should so love us as to come among us in Jesus and freely bear our sins on the cross in all their indescribable horror and shame leaves us no choice but to fall before him continually in thanksgiving, worship, and praise. "'Worthy is the Lamb, who was slain, to receive . . . honor and glory and praise'" (Rev. 5:12). "Thanks be to God for his indescribable gift" (2 Cor. 9:15). "To him who loves us and has freed us from our sins by his blood, . . . to him be glory and power for ever and ever! Amen" (Rev. 1:5–6).

But the work of Jesus for us is also an enormous encouragement as we seek to worship God, for he is not only an appropriate object of our worship but also a fellow-worshiper! During his earthly life, he offered a

Baptists in Worship

perfect response to the Father for us; and now as our ever-living High Priest (Heb. 2:17–18; 4:14–5:10; Luke 22:31), he stands with us in our response to the Father and offers on our behalf a perfect and fully acceptable human worship. He worships for us, and his perfect worship, like every aspect of his fully obedient humanity, is credited to us. This reality lifts the strain and sense of inadequacy from us as we draw near to God, struggling as we so often do with unbelief and our less than wholehearted devotion. We worship through him but also with him; hence, worship becomes a place where we can celebrate again with joy God's triumphant grace in Jesus Christ.

The Lord's Supper repeatedly renews these realities, as we contemplate in bread and wine the indescribable costliness of our redemption and the incomparable love that underlies it. Baptism confirms this focus as it points us to the amazing grace of God in the death and resurrection of Jesus. We revisit the cross and empty tomb, celebrating with exulting hearts this glorious God, who has mercy on sinners, pardoning their sins and accepting them as his children.

Third, God is Spirit. God is God a third time as the Holy Spirit. The Spirit is not represented in Scripture as a separate focus for our worship so much as the indispensable medium through whom we draw near to God; we worship by the Holy Spirit (Phil. 3:3; John 16:14; 1 Cor. 12:3). The Spirit's presence in worship is evidence that the grace of God really has entered our lives.

Baptism again embodies this coming of grace. The baptism of believers celebrates, in the midst of our worship, that through our faith in Christ God's grace really does embrace us. Further, as the presence of the kingdom of God which has already arrived (Matt. 12:28; John 3:1–8; Rom. 14:17), but which is still to appear in its fullness, the Spirit brings to our worship the joyful anticipation of worship in heaven (Rom. 14:17; 2 Cor. 5:5; Eph. 1:13–14).

In these ways, the Holy Spirit helps our worship; however, by virtue of being fully divine, the Spirit is also worthy of our adoration. The Spirit "with the Father and the Son together is worshiped and glorified" (Nicene-Constantinopolitan Creed).

Fourth, God is Father, Son, and Holy Spirit. In God the three persons are inseparably one. The God we worship is one as well as three, and three as well as one. This foundational Christian truth expresses the distinctiveness of God. He is the Father, Son, and Spirit, who has revealed himself personally and finally in human history. The triune

WE BAPTISTS

God is therefore distinct from the one God worshiped in Islam or Judaism. He is distinct from the multitude of manifestations, spirits, and incarnations of Hinduism. He is distinct from the all-encompassing One of Buddhism. He is distinct from the "self-as-god" of New Age religion as well as the personal idols which lurk in all our hearts.

God's three-in-oneness brings us to the edge of deep mystery. But that need not trouble us. It is the inevitable implication of God's being infinite. Indeed, without the presence of mystery, we would have reason to question the Bible's revelation. The medieval theologians expressed this by saying, "A God who can be fully comprehended is not the true God." In the end, we fall before the inexpressible wonder of the one true God. "Glory to the Father, and to the Son, and to the Holy Spirit, as it was in the beginning, is now, and shall be forever."

Worshiping in this way unites us with our Baptist forebears across the centuries, who, in turn, now join us in our worship from the other side of the curtain of death (Heb. 12:22–24; 12:1). We unite also with more than 42 million members of our worldwide, technicolor Baptist family of today. We unite finally in anticipation with that further company, including many of our own children, grandchildren, and as yet uncommitted friends who will in the future, by God's grace, bow before our Savior and take their places within the ages-long Baptist community which will hail Christ, as part of his glorified Bride, the Church, when He appears in glory.

HOW WE WORSHIP

In our first section, "Why We Worship," we have stood at almost every point within the whole company of the Lord's people of whatever denominational tradition. As we move to the "What?" and "How?" of worship, we discover a greater sense of our Baptist distinctiveness. But first we offer an important caveat. Anyone attempting to identify practices which are universal to Baptists is either unusually courageous or simply uninformed! Diversity has always been one of our glories, and the developments in the experience of worship worldwide during the last few years have only served to extend the range of possibilities. Contemporary worship now jostles for position beside traditional, charismatic beside reflective, and seeker-sensitive with alternative/generational. And this list is not exhaustive.

Baptists in Worship

MODELS OF WORSHIP

This variety, however, need not discourage us. No universal pattern of worship emerges from the Bible. In fact, it is possible to discern at least four fairly distinct models within Scripture.

First, the *didactic* model, the synagogue pattern, centers around the exposition of the law. This was the style in which Jesus was raised and which continued to shape early New Testament experience (James 2:2, "assembly," RSV; "synagogue," JB).

Second, the *liturgical* model, which was used in the temple worship of Israel, includes set forms and responses (see Ps. 136). The New Testament hints at worship formulae in a number of places (Eph. 5:14; Phil. 2:5–11; Col. 1:15–20; 1 Tim. 3:16; 1 Cor. 16:22b).

Third, the *sacramental* model reflects the sacrificial focus of much Old Testament worship and the centrality of the Lord's Supper in New Testament experience (Acts 2:42, 46; 20:7; 1 Cor. 11:23–34).

Fourth, the *charismatic* model expresses the worship gifts listed in 1 Cor. 12:8–12 (Acts 11:27–28; 21:8–11) with Old Testament anticipations (Num. 11:26–29; 1 Sam.10:12–13).

Perhaps we might identify a fifth, the *festival* model, expressed in the annual feasts of Israel, which brought the whole people of God together in celebration (Exod. 23:14–19a). Jesus' ministry was significantly shaped by this pattern (Luke 2:41–50; John 2:13, 23; 7:37; 13:1; 19:14). There is a hint in Acts that the primitive church continued to observe special times of celebrative gathering (Acts 20:16).

In practice, we are not required to choose between these biblical models. Most Baptist churches consciously combine several of these patterns. The diversity of the Scriptures, however, should cause us to pause before enthroning one particular style as "the biblical form of worship." In the wisdom of God, we have been given a freedom to allow worship the flexibility it has needed over the centuries to adapt to the huge diversity of cultures and of historical experiences which the ages have presented.

A word of caution is appropriate. When due tribute is paid to the diversities within the Bible itself and the varieties of instinct and experience within today's congregations around the world, we need to be careful lest differences over styles of worship endanger our spiritual unity in the one Body of Christ. One of Christianity's supremely attractive features in the early centuries was its offer of authentic, loving community

53

amid the often lonely and fragmented Greco-Roman world. Christianity taught people with great cultural diversity to worship "with one heart and mouth . . . the God and Father of our Lord Jesus Christ," thus bringing "praise to God" (Rom. 15:6–7).

Ours is also a sharply divided world. It would be tragic indeed if in the church, and even within single congregations, we simply reflect the social, racial, and generational divisions of our atomized communities. It would perhaps be even more tragic, because of divisions over worship styles, should we cease to be the authentic bearers of the message of reconciliation which our broken world so desperately needs. In the light of these dangers it is appropriate to explore certain common tendencies in Baptist worship.

THE WORSHIPING COMMUNITY

If Baptists possess universal distinctives, one of them is the stress on the local congregation. Thomas Helwys's confession in 1611 expresses that perspective memorably: "though in respect of Christ the Church be one, yet it consisteth of divers particular congregations, . . . every of which congregation, though they be but two or three, have Christ given them, with all the means of their salvation [and] are the body of Christ, and a whole Church. And therefore may, and ought, when they are come together, to pray, prophesy, break bread, and administer in all the holy ordinances" (art. 11).

For Baptists, worship is primarily the worship of the congregation to which the individual believer belongs. Historically, a significant contributory factor to this stress on the worshiping community was a revulsion against the hierarchical worship of the medieval church. Under that pattern, the laity could enter God's presence only through the worship offered on their behalf by the priest. In recovering true Christian worship, the Protestant Reformers championed the priesthood of all believers, the conviction that every Christian is a true priest of God and ministers along with other priests in God's presence through worship and prayer. Baptists have been in the vanguard in celebrating this crucial biblical insight. Several things follow from this concept of the worshiping community.

First, while personal worship in "your room" (Matt. 6:6) is a practice that needs no defense among Baptists, the worship focus is a corporate experience, commonly on Sundays, when the whole congregation gathers.

Baptists in Worship

Second, this experience needs to involve the congregation. Undoubtedly in most Baptist congregations worldwide, the pastor has a leading role in planning and leading worship services. But passages such as 1 Corinthians 12:4–12, with its metaphor of a body with complementary, functioning members, are significant. Not all Baptist congregations feel the constraint to encourage a charismatic (in the narrower sense of the word) expression of the gifts of the Holy Spirit, though some do. Where Baptist worship, however, consists entirely of the leadership of the ordained minister, with no other voices heard apart from those lifted in congregational praise, that church may have departed from traditional Baptist convictions.

Third, worship needs the setting of deep mutual concern. The focus in the worship service should be not merely upward toward God, but also outward towards fellow members. Put another way, the God we worship is discerned, not merely as exalted infinitely over us, but also as disclosing himself through his children, our brothers and sisters in Christ, seated around us. "But the greatest . . . is love" (1 Cor. 13:13) has its application to worship, as to all other areas of our Christian experience. Jesus even teaches that being in dispute with a fellow worshiper effectively invalidates our worship (Matt. 5:21–25). Paul is arguably making the same point in 1 Corinthians 11:27–34. We pass judgment on ourselves when we partake of the Lord's Supper without "discernment of the Body," that is, without recognizing the seriousness of tolerating disunity within Christ's Body, the church community. True Baptist worship is Body-of-Christ worship.

ORDER AND FREEDOM

The heart of our stress on the primacy of the local congregation is the promise of Jesus, "For where two or three come together in my name, there am I with them" (Matt. 28:20). The congregational context of worship and the competence of the local church for ordering its affairs both derive from the conviction that, as it meets, the church experiences the presence of the risen Lord.

This principle should bring to our worship a sense of freshness, even excitement, as we come together in the presence of the living Lord. This need not imply an absence of concern for order in worship. In practice, Baptists across the centuries have found a Spirit-given appropriateness in prayerfully giving shape and order to their worship experience. But where services are so tightly structured that they move forward with a leaden, even boring predictability, and there is no discernible room for any movement of God among us, we have again violated our basic congregational principle. At the heart of worship is nothing less than a meeting with the risen Lord Jesus—surely the most renewing, stimulating, and exciting experience available to humankind!

As we enter the third millennium, this concern for a proper freedom in our worship has several new and significant contexts. We live in a world where older lines of division are breaking down. Many churches are experiencing the thrill of welcoming new worshipers who have no traditional Baptist or even Christian roots. Their needs and expectations are different, yet they, too, long to worship. We need to find ways to listen to and authentically embrace them.

Ours is also a shrinking world. The combination of the communications revolution with the unprecedented movement of peoples around the globe means that churches, particularly in urban centers, are increasingly racially and culturally diverse. These are, in some ways, the congregations of the future. This reality opens exciting prospects for Baptist worship. The *World Praise* songbook launched at the BWA Congress in Buenos Aires in 1995 represents an important first wave of that multicultural worship which beckons excitingly on the horizon and which will so remarkably prepare its participants for the multicultural worship of heaven (Dan. 7:14; Rev. 7:13).

THE WORD OF GOD

Baptists are Bible people. In *What Baptists Stand For*, Henry Cook writes: "It is this emphasis on the supremacy of the New Testament in all matters of faith and practice that constitutes the basis of the Baptist position" (p. 13).

We have already referred to the four-hour diets of Bible reading and exposition in the 1609 Baptist congregation in Amsterdam. Although today's length of services varies greatly, from one hour in some Western congregations to three hours and more in many churches in Eastern Europe, Asia, and Africa, the instinct for the rule of Scripture remains. Thus, worship properly begins with a scriptural call to worship expressing God's initiative and leadership. The public reading of a passage or passages of Scripture is an important moment in the service, and responsive or unison readings may also be included.

Baptists in Worship

The most obvious way in which God's speaking through his Word is reflected in Baptist worship lies in the sermon. Properly understood, the sermon is a fundamental part of worship and even arguably one of its most sacred moments, since it is a time when God speaks directly to us. The challenge to the preacher is enormous. Sermons which are poorly prepared or sloppily delivered, which lack depth of understanding of the biblical text, or which are devoid of application to the life experience of the hearers are a violation of this high and holy moment in worship. But prayerfully and responsibly handled, the preaching of the Word can represent, for a listening congregation, a moment of overwhelming significance, as they are brought into the very presence of God, hear his voice, and are encountered by him in his grace and glory.

An important concomitant of this commitment to the Word of God is an emphasis on lay training. Many Baptist churches make provision for Christian education, at very least for the young. Where it extends to cover all age-groups, it is designed to give lay members access to a vital, working knowledge of the Scriptures in their relationship to our everyday lives.

PSALMS, HYMNS, AND SPIRITUAL SONGS

"My heart is steadfast, O God; I will sing and make music" (Ps. 108:1). The psalmist reflects a fundamental instinct of the human spirit before the glory and goodness of God. Singing and making music were central in biblical worship, whether as the spontaneous celebration of a Miriam (Exod. 15), the choir-led praises of the temple (Neh. 12), the "psalms, hymns and spiritual songs" of the new covenant (Col. 3:16), or the ecstatic praises of the heavenly hosts (Rev. 5:13; 7:10).

Our earliest Baptists were a little reticent in this matter, preferring to major on biblical exposition to the virtual exclusion of all else. The passing of the centuries, however, has brought an appreciation of the fundamental place of congregational praise and the ministry of music generally. Baptists have been among the major hymn writers and compilers of hymns, such as Benjamin Keach and John Rippon and in our own period B. B. McKinney, William J. Reynolds, David Peacock, and Graham Kendrick. Churches operating with multiple staffs regularly include a minister of music in recognition of the elemental role of music, both choral and instrumental, in the enrichment of Christian worship. The significant explosion of new songs written in the last thirty years has contributed greatly to the renewal of Baptist worship in many places. Sadly, at times, tensions have developed around new-versus-old musical styles and lyrics. Happily, in other places, a sensitive, mature blending of the two streams has brought deep enrichment and new relevance.

THE ORDINANCES

Baptists have always recognized the importance of the actions of Jesus in instituting the two gospel ordinances of baptism and the Lord's Supper. In order to avoid embarrassing nonpartaking congregants, the Supper is sometimes tacked on or added as an after service. Sadly, this practice can demean its significance. Sensitivity to nonparticipants' feelings is a healthy instinct, but it is possible to be overly sensitive. We ought not to underestimate the evangelistic potential of the Lord's Supper itself, both in declaring the gospel and in providing an opportunity for response to it as the elements of the Supper become tangible vehicles of a personal embrace of the Christ to whom they point. Both these ordinances point directly to Christ and bind the church ever more surely to him.

"CONCERNING THE COLLECTION"

Biblical worship found a significant place for the presentation of tithes and offerings. In both testaments, the response to God's grace and goodness called for tangible, thoughtful, and sacrificial response in money or kind (Gen. 14:20; Lev. 27:30; Mal. 3:10; Matt. 6:2–4; 1 Cor. 16:1–4). Baptists have consistently affirmed this. Today, annual budgets are common, and many churches have a stewardship committee to foster and monitor the giving of the congregation and to keep stewardship principles before the members. The presentation of the gifts of the people, often on the Communion table, is a high and meaningful moment in Baptist worship services and for many provides an opportunity to share in the extension of God's kingdom. The trend in some Western churches towards monthly, or even annual, giving may serve to blunt the force of this weekly act of worship and commitment.

Baptists in Worship

"LIFTING UP HOLY HANDS"

Priestly ministry in the Bible implied the offering of prayer (Heb. 5:1–3, 7–10; see 1 Sam. 12:23). As an expression of the priesthood of the entire congregation, intercessory prayers have traditionally been a significant part of our worship. Although usually offered by the ordained minister or other worship leader, they represent the combined prayers of the whole church and should be structured in such a way that the congregation can meaningfully participate. Paul's plea for a proper width in our Christian concerns is to the point here: "I urge . . . intercession . . . be made for everyone—for kings and all those in authority" (1 Tim. 2:1–2). At this point, our worship needs to touch the range of the needs of the congregation and also to embrace the global community in its brokenness and need. Appropriately led, the intercessory prayer is a deeply significant happening in a Baptist worship service.

THE OVERFLOWS OF WORSHIP

Our worship is appropriately focused and expressed in corporate services within a church building or other meeting place. But since God is Lord of all of life, ascribing worth to him can never be limited to a single place or to a single time in the week. Authentic Christian worship recognizes three ways in which our concern for God's worthiness overflows from congregational services.

First, as Jesus notes, there is a need to "go into your room, close the door and pray to your Father . . . in secret" (Matt. 6:6). He himself was a model of this private devotion (Luke 11:1; Matt. 14:23; Heb. 5:7). Baptists, like other Christians, have long recognized the call to "sing and make music in your heart " (Eph. 5:19b) and "pray continually" (1 Thess. 5:17). Quiet times are regularly encouraged among Baptists as a significant element in Christian discipleship. Provided they avoid the dangers of legalism, they can represent a significant quickening of our relationship to God and help to infuse the congregational worship experience with depth and reality. But for many Baptists, the most profound experience in prayer may be in the presence of other believers, as at a riverbank in Ghana or in an early-morning church prayer meeting in South Korea.

Second, as disciples of Christ, we are called to bear his name in the world, to be his "witnesses" (Acts 1:8). H. Wheeler Robinson aptly entitled this "the prophethood of all believers." Sharing the gospel has always been recognized by Baptists as a sacred duty. The Baptist Union of Great Britain and Ireland, among others, includes the phrase "to bear personal witness to the Lord Jesus Christ" within its Statement of Principle. The act of sharing the gospel is replete with worship significance.

The Bible teaches that all people are by nature worshipers (Rom. 1:25). "We must worship God or an idol" (Martin Luther). As fallen beings, we worship false gods. Accordingly, when the gospel summons people to repentance, it is calling them to renounce these idols in their hearts and to begin to worship and serve the one true God. Put another way, a concern for God's honor in the world will inevitably express itself, among other things, in a concern for world evangelization. The dishonor rendered to God by the idols worshiped in the hearts of non-Christians will be relieved, and true honor will be brought to God, as they repent and call upon him through the Lord Jesus Christ.

Baptists, by their huge contribution to the global spread of the gospel, through William Carey, Adoniram Judson, and their multitude of successors, have thereby shown a heart for God's honor in the world; their worship has overflowed. Similarly, the passion for evangelism reflected in great Baptist preachers like C. H. Spurgeon, Alexander Maclaren, George W. Truett, Billy Graham, Billy Kim, and Nilson Fanini is at heart a yearning for the glory of God in the world. It is an authentic overflow of worship. True worshipers are witnesses.

Third, our worship overflows as it touches our everyday lives. Paul urges the Colossians, "Whatever you do, work at it with all your heart, as working for the Lord. . . . It is the Lord Christ you are serving" (Col. 3:23–24). The Lord is honored; hence, worship is brought him, as we fulfill our daily responsibilities to the best of our ability for him. This very significant principle extends worship, at one stroke, to the whole of our lives. Hence, our weekdays in the marketplace, home, or community stand alongside Sunday in the sanctuary as worship times, as do our leisure moments. "So shall no part of day or night from sacredness be free" (Horatius Bonar's hymn, "Fill Thou My Life, O Lord My God"). In this connection, the most common New Testament word for worship can also be translated "service" (Rom. 12:1; Rev. 22:3).

This holistic understanding of Christian discipleship has found significant reflection in Baptist life over the centuries. It is expressed in the strong affirmation of lay ministry and in the instinct for human dignity, religious liberty, and social justice which has claimed the public arena as a basic sphere for Christian ministry alongside the

Baptists in Worship

church and the sanctuary. "Is not this the kind of fasting I have chosen: to loose the chains of injustice and . . . to set the oppressed free and . . . to share your food with the hungry" (Isa. 58:6–7)? This recognition of the breadth of worship is a wonderfully liberating truth for laypeople who may not have the time to involve themselves in church-based forms of service. It is a call not just to attend worship services but to adopt a worship lifestyle.

CONCLUSION

As we enter a new millennium, the summons is unchanged: "'Worship the Lord your God, and serve him only'" (Matt. 4:10). Baptists can face the challenge of the future with confidence. The Lord has shown us who he is. He draws us into worship. Glory be to his name. He has also helped us to shape our worship response. We know, in part at least, what he wants us to do in worship.

As Baptist believers, we have a great past to inspire us and a wonderful, international community to which to belong. We have a sense of high-touch community, which will prove increasingly significant. We have an instinct for freedom and flexibility to help us to face the challenges of tomorrow's world. But our confidence is rooted finally in the Lord and Head of the Church, who is among us and who promises his continuing presence, until that moment, determined from eternity, when he who came will come again "with great power and glory" (Mark 13:26). Then the worship we now offer, which is the greatest privilege we share and the highest activity of which we are capable, will give place to the worship of heaven, and with all God's people, from all the churches and all the ages, we will fall before him in worship. "'To him who sits on the throne and to the Lamb be praise and honor and glory and power, for ever and ever! . . . Amen'" (Rev. 5:13–14).

CHAPTER FIVE

Baptist Church Life
and Leadership

OUR LIVES ARE WRAPPED UP IN OUR OWN STORIES AND THE stories of people in our own land. It is not easy for one Baptist Christian to imagine that he or she is part of a fellowship of 42 million baptized believers in almost two hundred nations. Many persons go through life as if they were the center of creation. Such provincialism makes one's perspective unreliable. You, as one Baptist person, are in one congregation and nation that is part of 191 Baptist unions and conventions throughout the world—a global family.

Ideas shared herein remind us that we are part of a larger narrative and that God wants to break into our story. To admit that God is the central actor in human history gives us a new perspective. Our stories would be pointless without the Author of the story. Good news! God, the often unrecognized Presence, desires to enter our story and take us beyond it. As we read about church life and work, think of how the biblical story of redemption shapes and instructs church leadership today.

The starting place for examining Baptist church life and leadership is the biblical foundations. This is especially true since some churches face confusion. Certain congregations have followed secular models rather than biblical teachings. One such model is from the business community, where leaders market products and manage institutions. The military serves as another model. Various religious groups have relied on militaristic power to make converts and force their faith on people. Christians fell to this temptation during the Crusades of the

Baptist Church Life and Leadership

Middle Ages. Entertainment has influenced Baptist worship styles. In some churches, leaders have depended on showmanship to attract people. Similarly, sports (athletics) has appealed to some churches that thrive on competition.

In certain parts of the world, Christians meet informally for Bible study, prayer, and fellowship and yet call themselves a church. A lay preacher in Zambia has seventeen congregations in remote villages. He visits these mission points infrequently, and they are not well formed or duly organized as congregations. Is a house meeting of Chinese believers a church? Turning to the Scriptures can help us to overcome misguided views of church definition, life, and leadership.

The biblical word for the New Testament church means "those who are called," assembled before God, and under his rule. The church is made up of persons who are called by God to salvation. It is not a club which people join for benefits, but those called by God who respond to God's grace. Jesus Christ is the foundation of the church, and his Spirit forms the basis of fellowship in a church. Paul the apostle wrote: "For just as the body is one and has many members, and all the members of the body, though many, are one body, so it is with Christ. For by one Spirit we were all baptized into one body—Jews or Greeks, slaves or free—and were all made to drink of one Spirit" (1 Cor. 12:12–13, RSV).

Some readers might wonder what distinguishes Baptists' priorities from other Christians' understandings of church life and leadership. We share in common with certain other groups of Christians beliefs like salvation by grace through faith; believer's baptism by immersion; a regenerate church membership; congregational polity; the priesthood of all believers; even the tenet of separation of church and state. Basic to these understandings is a prior principle: the individual's capacity for direct access to God. Some Baptists have called this ideal the competency of the soul (ability of a person) for a God relationship. Non-Baptist denominations may cherish one or more of these common doctrines. The Baptist distinctive may be found in the way all of these cherished beliefs fit together.

Each of these Baptist beliefs rests upon the principle of an individual's capacity to experience God. Once a person responds by faith to God's gift of salvation in Jesus Christ, obedience requires that he/she receive baptism into a local fellowship of believers. Duly constituted congregations of baptized members freely govern themselves, but not through a network of some religious hierarchy. Each believer is a priest, both before God for oneself and by caring for fellow believers and for persons in the world for whom Christ died.

WE BAPTISTS

Once you are a member of a particular community of believers, how can you share church life and leadership? Beyond that, how do Baptist congregations work in obedience to God's plan for world evangelization? It is to such issues that our attention now turns.

GOD'S SALVATION PLAN

Baptists believe that salvation from sin to eternal life precedes church membership. Paul wrote to Christians in Ephesus, "For by grace you have been saved through faith, and this is not your own doing, it is the gift of God—not because of works, lest any man should boast. For we are his workmanship, created in Christ Jesus for good works, which God prepared beforehand, that we should walk in them" (Eph. 2:8–10). God's initiative is his elective grace. Our response is personal faith, the means by which we accept his gift of eternal life through Jesus Christ's sacrificial death on the cross. Though we are not created by our good works, we are created for good works.

These words in Ephesians are the heart of the gospel. God's plan is simple and basic, yet people through the centuries have sought to add to it. For example, when Paul and Barnabas preached the Good News (gospel) to Gentiles, a group in the Jerusalem church, whom we call Judaizers, were critical (Acts 15:1–5). They believed that Gentiles had to become Jewish proselytes and be circumcised in order to receive salvation in Christ. Their position required faith plus works, not God's grace through faith alone. Such spiritual confusion caused a major conflict in the primitive church, which was resolved at the Jerusalem Conference (Acts 15).

The basic meaning of grace is a gift of unmerited favor. One of the New Testament verbs translated "to forgive" comes from the root of grace. It is not God's desire that anyone should perish, but that all persons everywhere should repent and receive eternal life (2 Pet. 3:9). His gift is free for all who will receive it. Some denominations tend to add requirements and expand on God's gift; for example, baptismal regeneration in traditions requiring baptism for salvation, the teaching authority of the pope in the Roman Catholic Church, and charismatic gifts in some traditions and congregations.

When a person trusts Jesus Christ, that one is assured of eternal life. Yet the New Testament teaches that salvation is an event, a process, and a consummation. When believers in New Testament times experienced temptations and trials, they were told: your "salvation is nearer . . . now

64

Baptist Church Life and Leadership

than when . . . [you] first believed" (Rom. 13:11). Various early Christians thought conversion was the end, but soon learned it was the front end of salvation. Paul reminded them and us: "Work out your own salvation with fear and trembling" (Phil. 2:12). God honors such obedience with his constant care and powerful presence.

Baptists hold that once a person is genuinely born again, a maturing process is involved. The beginning we call regeneration or a new birth from above. Jesus' conversation with Nicodemus (John 3:3–7) made clear that regeneration is a spiritual birth. Just as one is born into physical life, relationships, and responsibilities, spiritual birth is essential. Baptism shows that the old self must die; a new spiritual and moral self is born.

Regeneration requires discipling and living on the road toward righteousness. This living out the Christian journey is called sanctification. With the formation of a Christlike character come choices, temptations, failures, heartaches, sorrows, and joys. That is the faith journey; so Christ gave us the church as a company of fellow believers. Moreover, God gives us his Spirit, just as he endowed believers in Bible times (John 14:16–17a; Eph. 1:13b–14). Paul wrote that a Christian's body becomes a very "temple" of the Holy Spirit (1 Cor. 6:19).

Ultimately, salvation points to glorification after this earthly journey. The Bible teaches that beyond death is resurrection and judgment. Glory implies the time of receiving our reward in heaven, after our bodily resurrection (Rom. 8:23; Eph. 1:14). All Christians who are regenerated will be with God in heaven. But the extent of one's rewards will be determined by one's faithfulness on earth (Matt. 25:14–23).

Joining a congregation of Christian believers is not the same as salvation. After one first believes in Jesus Christ, one's obedience requires sharing membership in a community of Christian believers. The New Testament suggests that the church is an organism *(koinonia)*—"the body of Christ"—with an inner life of its own. It is structured also as an organization *(ecclesia)*—believers "called out" of sin to function on mission in the world. We learn from the first Christians that Baptists need to be a people with a purpose, sent on mission for God.

SENT ON MISSION

Jesus understood that he was not on a journey for his own sake but was sent to minister. Luke records Jesus' saying: "'I must preach the good news of the kingdom of God to the other cities also; for I was sent for this purpose'" (Luke 4:43). Jesus ministered as one sent from God and instructed his disciples about what this meant to them: "'He who receives you receives me, and he who receives me receives him who sent me'" (Matt. 10:40). Jesus' idea of being sent by God likely reflected the usage in Jewish rabbinic literature of his day of the word *šaliaḥ*, meaning envoy, agent, or ambassador.

As Jesus was the envoy of God, he appointed disciples to be his ambassadors. According to Luke 9, Jesus sent out the twelve; and according to Luke 10, he sent out seventy. Whatever the relationship between these stories, they show Jesus as sending. The passage we call "the Great Commission" (Matt. 28:18–20) is an extension of that sending. What is involved in this sending? It is to make disciples (evangelism) and to teach (truth).

A world-changing mission is the author's vision in Luke-Acts. Luke began with a broad overview of God's plan for Jesus' birth and earthly ministry (chs. 1–3). Following Jesus' temptation, his missionary challenge in relation to Judaism and the Roman Empire was lived out in Galilee and other Palestinian areas and ended in Jerusalem. Jesus' post-resurrection words in Acts 1:8 describe the church's mission: "'But you shall receive power when the Holy Spirit has come upon you, and you shall be my witnesses in Jerusalem and in all Judaea and Samaria and to the end of the earth.'" The first task of redemption was the work of Jesus. The second mission is to be undertaken by witnesses who are the apostles of Jesus Christ.

The apostles were central characters in the primitive church. Paul became an apostle because of his Christ-vision conversion experience on the road to Damascus. His epistles often provide defense for his apostleship. His ministry was fulfilling the Great Commission as an apostle of Jesus Christ.

Philippians 2 is a description of God's sending Jesus. His ministry is captured in an early Christian hymn quoted by the apostle Paul. Christ Jesus left the richness of glory to be born in humble circumstances, serve humanity, die on the cross, and be raised from the dead. Paul appeals to the church of Philippi to be like Jesus.

Church life involves being sent by Jesus Christ. We are people of the Great Commission. The act of baptism identifies believers with Christ's redemptive mission—making disciples in all the world. The Great Commission also says to teach. Church life is to lead people from the darkness of ignorance into the light of truth. The church is to teach people

Baptist Church Life and Leadership

"'to observe all that I have commanded you'" (Matt. 28:20). Just as there is baptism, so there is an ethical content of the gospel of Jesus Christ. As the church's textbook, the Bible guides Christian character formation, personal choices, and conduct in the community of faith. This new way of life is lived out in service for God.

SERVICE FOR GOD

The word "servant" is important to church leaders because it was important to Jesus. He saw himself as taking the role of the Suffering Servant in Isaiah 53. Mark 10:45 presents Jesus' reflection on himself: "'For the Son of Man also came not to be served but to serve, and to give his life as a ransom for many.'" The Last Supper was a drama that illustrated the servanthood of Jesus. The climax of the drama was when Jesus washed the disciples' feet. He took the role of a lowly household servant by washing the feet of dinner guests.

The primitive Christian church soon interpreted Jesus' ministry in terms of the Suffering Servant of Isaiah. The hymn in Philippians 2 declares that Jesus took "the form of a servant." Seeing that Jesus lived as a servant, early Christians began to describe themselves as servants and to seek service. When the seven were chosen (Acts 6:1–6), they were chosen to serve. Some interpreters hold that these were the first deacons. The argument for the seven's being the first deacons has been that the Greek word for "deacon" is *diakonos*, which means "servant."

Paul claimed the status of servant. He opened some of his epistles by claiming to be an apostle but in others (Romans and Philippians) claimed that he was a servant *(doulos)* of Jesus Christ. He used "servant" as a word of commendation for others when alluding to Phoebe in Romans 16:1 *(diakonos)* and to Epaphras in Colossians 4:12 *(doulos)*.

The priesthood of believers is part of this servanthood of Jesus' disciples. According to 1 Peter 2:4–10 Jesus is the stone that the builders rejected but that God chose as a precious cornerstone. This sounds very much like the hymn in Philippians 2, in which at last God exalts his servant Son. The rejection in 1 Peter is probably a servant image. The result is that Christians are "a chosen race, a royal priesthood, a holy nation, God's own people." This priesthood is not, however, for the Christian's glory but to "declare the wonderful deeds of him who called you out of darkness into his marvelous light." Hence, as priests

Christians are to serve by declaring the wonderful deeds of Christ. For Christians the rule of priesthood is not over others but among them. We are priests to one another.

The strong emphasis on servanthood in Jesus and the apostolic church is important for the life and leadership of the church, for leaders are those who serve. According to S. F. Winward in *The Pattern of the Church: A Baptist View,* edited by Alec Gilmore, the church gets its servant, shepherding, prophetic, and priestly tasks from Jesus himself. The basis of church leadership is not so much ability as availability. The chief quality of church leaders is not their authority but their spirit of servanthood. The church's finest hours have been those when it served the world, and its darkest hours have been when it sought status rather than servanthood.

The church's service includes worship, or the "sacrifice of praise to God" (Heb. 13:15), proclamation, or declaring "the wonderful deeds of him who called you" (1 Pet. 2:9), and ministry, or serving the disadvantaged (Heb. 13:16). So evangelism is the work of a servant, not a salesperson. Feeding the hungry, helping the poor, and assisting the oppressed are acts of servants (Luke 4:17–19).

The church and its leaders need to heed the admonition of Jesus, "'Truly, truly, I say to you, a servant is not greater than his master'" (John 13:16). If Jesus was the servant, the church is a servant community. As Jesus was a servant, the legitimate work of church leaders is to serve others rather than to glorify themselves. Such obedient endeavor is made possible by the presence, guidance, and empowerment of God's Spirit (2 Cor. 4:7).

POWER OF THE HOLY SPIRIT

The word "spirit" describes the vital center of church life. Often the New Testament used the term "Holy Spirit" rather than "spirit." Whatever word one uses, it needs to refer to God's empowering Spirit rather than confusing "spirit" with enthusiastic activity or mere emotionalism. God's Spirit is the "Comforter" or "Counselor" to whom the Gospel of John (14:16, 26; 15:26; 16:7) refers.

As with salvation, mission, and servanthood, Jesus is the source of our thinking about the Spirit as central to church life and work. The story of the virginal conception is the starting point. Luke 1:35 portrays an angel telling Mary: "The Holy Spirit will come upon you, and the power of the Most

Baptist Church Life and Leadership

High will overshadow you; therefore the child to be born will be called holy, the Son of God." Jesus' special conception was by the Holy Spirit.

The Spirit was important throughout Jesus' life and ministry (John 3:34). The Gospel of Mark tells about Jesus' baptism: "And when he came up out of the water, immediately he saw the heavens opened and the Spirit descending upon him like a dove; and a voice came from heaven, 'Thou art my beloved son; with thee I am well pleased'" (1:10). Mark records that the Spirit then "drove him out into the wilderness" (1:12).

The Gospel of Luke stresses the role of the Spirit in the life and ministry of Jesus. From the wilderness "Jesus returned in the power of the Spirit into Galilee" (4:14). Teaching in the synagogue in Nazareth, Jesus quoted Isaiah and said, "'Today this scripture has been fulfilled in your hearing'" (4:17–21). The quotation from Isaiah began, "The Spirit of the Lord is upon me. . . ." Luke also recalls that Jesus "rejoiced in the Holy Spirit" (10:21). Three of the Gospels, Matthew, Mark, and Luke, tell the story of the transfiguration of Jesus, Moses, and Elijah. Although the Spirit is not mentioned, the words used at Jesus' baptism ("Thou art my beloved son") are repeated.

Jesus claimed that his miracles were by the Spirit of God. Jesus announced that it was "'by the finger of God'" that "'he cast out demons'" (Luke 11:20). The "finger of God" (see Exod. 8:19) referred to the Spirit of God. The context of the saying was the charge that Jesus used evil spirits such as Beelzebul to cast out demons. Jesus instead claimed that it was by the Spirit of God, not by an evil spirit, that he cast out demons.

When Jesus warned about the unpardonable sin (Matt. 12:31–32), he clearly stated that the unpardonable sin was speaking against the Holy Spirit, a greater blasphemy than speaking against the Son of Man. Jesus told his disciples to depend upon the Holy Spirit when they faced persecution (Luke 12:11–12). Luke places this right after the treatment of the unpardonable sin. There is obviously a contrast between the evil spirits and the Holy Spirit.

The Gospel of John adds a future dimension to the work of the Holy Spirit. When Jesus is gone, the disciples will be taught and will remember because of "the Counselor, the Holy Spirit, whom the Father will send in my name" (14:26). The Spirit was Jesus' companion during his life, and he promised that the Spirit would be the disciples' counselor. The Spirit directed, blessed, and empowered Jesus.

The primitive church began its work with the power and blessing of the Holy Spirit. Peter's sermon at Pentecost began with a quotation from

Joel: """And in the last days it shall be, God declares, that I will pour out my Spirit upon all flesh . . ."""" (Acts 2:17). Prior to Pentecost, the Spirit occasionally endowed special persons, such as the Old Testament prophets. At Pentecost, Peter said that the prophecy of Joel had been fulfilled and the Spirit poured out. Now the Spirit has become universal and constant. Because of the Spirit, people of all languages heard the gospel from commoners out of Galilee. The church was born in the power of the Spirit.

During the early years of the church, Christians began to realize that they had gifts from the Spirit. The apostle Paul chided the Galatian Christians by asking, "Did you receive the Spirit by works of the law, or by hearing with faith?" (Gal. 3:2). He also reminded them of the true fruit of the Spirit in Christian behavior (5:22–24). Paul wrote specifically about spiritual gifts (1 Cor. 12–14). "Now there are varieties of gifts, but the same Spirit" (12:4). After indicating many gifts of the Spirit (12:8–10, 28–30), Paul continued with the chapter on love (ch. 13), the true test of one's living in the Spirit, and finally dealt with prophecy (ch. 14).

Paul reminded the Philippian Christians of their "participation in the Spirit" (Phil. 2:1). He implied that when one is in the Spirit, a person will have the mind of Christ, which is seen in the hymn he quoted (2:6–11). The church of the New Testament was a church of the Spirit. While there were the apostles and the seven, there were other leaders who had "participation in the Spirit" (Phil. 2:1). Stephen, the first Christian martyr, was called "a man full of faith and of the Holy Spirit" (Acts 6:5). Philip, also one of the seven, had four daughters who prophesied (Acts 21:9). The Spirit led the life of the primitive church and inspired the leaders. Although today's churches are separated in time, culture, and distance from the primitive church, our need for reliance upon God's Spirit is much the same.

SHARED MINISTRY

The New Testament shows how leadership emerged in different settings. It does not specify one polity, or means of governance. Offices and organizations changed over time, according to needs, settings, and new situations. We see clearly two types of leaders emerging in Acts and the Pauline epistles, including the pastoral letters. Charismatic leaders were gifted by God for certain actions to benefit a given congregation. As churches developed along institutional lines, more formal offices appeared.

Baptist Church Life and Leadership

In Acts 6:1–6, the twelve apostles confined their tasks to preaching and teaching and appointed seven "helpers" when a special need arose. Later, in Acts 11:30, 15:22, and 21:18, a group of elders (*presbyteroi*) emerged. Prophets, whom Luke in Acts 15:22 calls "leading men among the brethren," presided in various worship situations (Acts 13:1–3).

The Jerusalem church, according to Acts, was first led by the twelve apostles. In time, a council of elders emerged with James, the Lord's half-brother, as leader. Various designations and practices appear in the Pauline writings. In 1 Thessalonians 5:12–13 and 1 Corinthians 16:15–18, Paul addressed certain leaders but gave them no title. Elsewhere, all believers who assembled in worship to minister to one another were addressed (1 Cor. 12:4–7; Rom. 12:3–8). In another letter, Paul addressed "all the saints" who are with "the bishops and deacons," official officers in New Testament churches (Phil. 1:1). In writing to Timothy, he added "elders" to his list of leaders (1 Tim. 5:17–22).

Besides the appearance in the New Testament of gifted persons with offices such as "apostles," "prophets," and "teachers" (1 Cor. 12:28; Eph. 4:11), household settings apparently shaped the pattern of life and social interaction of the first Christians. The head of an ancient household who extended hospitality to a community of believers exercised some authority over the whole group and assumed responsibility for the church in his or her house. The needs of Christians in varied settings required tailor-made leadership.

In the New Testament each church was seemingly self-governing. Its primary officers were pastors or bishops and deacons, who, along with members of the congregation, shared the ministry of the church. Each believer, baptized into the fellowship, had work to do. Paul reminded members of one congregation that they were "God's fellow workers" (2 Cor. 6:1, NIV). All church members, official leaders and rank-and-file members alike, bore responsibility for one another. That is the basis for shared ministry in today's congregations.

RISK OF SUFFERING AND SACRIFICE

As Christians seek to obey God's call in keeping with Christ's mission, suffering and sacrifice may be required. Suffering and sacrifice are terms describing potential hardships and risks which church leaders may face. Christian leaders do what needs to be done. Leading God's flock is hard work because one is dealing constantly with people.

WE BAPTISTS

Holding up divine ideals and promoting change may provoke resistance or resentment, even persecution. We should, accordingly, admit that leading God's people is a costly, sometimes dangerous, enterprise.

Jesus certainly faced suffering and sacrifice. This was part of his fulfilling Isaiah's prophecy of the Suffering Servant (Isa. 53). Luke's story of the Last Supper includes Jesus' saying to the disciples, "'I have earnestly desired to eat this passover with you before I suffer'" (22:15, RSV). The Last Supper of the broken bread and the wine was symbolic of his broken body and spilled blood to make possible salvation for humankind.

His death on the cross was suffering, but it was also a sacrifice. Mark 10:45 ties the themes of servanthood, suffering, and sacrifice together: "'For the Son of man also came not to be served but to serve, and to give his life as a ransom for many.'" Luke also tells of the conversation of Jesus on the road to Emmaus with some disciples who were unaware that they were talking with Jesus. Jesus chided them, "'O foolish men, and slow of heart to believe all that the prophets have spoken! Was it not necessary that the Christ should suffer these things and enter into his glory?'" (Luke 24:25–26). Jesus understood his mission as a sacrificial endeavor, fulfilling Isaiah's suffering servant image.

The disciples had learned their lesson by the time of Pentecost. They made the connection between Isaiah and Jesus. Peter's sermon at Pentecost referred to the fact that Jesus "'was killed by the hands of lawless men'" (Acts 2:23). In Acts 3, Peter was more direct: "'But what God foretold by the mouth of all the prophets, that his Christ should suffer, he thus fulfilled'" (Acts 3:18). Paul tied the ideas of suffering and substitution together. He wrote: "While we were still weak, at the right time Christ died for the ungodly" (Rom. 5:6). Again, Paul wrote: "But God shows his love for us in that while we were yet sinners Christ died for us" (Rom. 5:8).

The primitive church leaders connected Jesus' sufferings and sacrifice with their own mission. After some apostles had been in prison, they left the council "rejoicing that they were counted worthy to suffer dishonor for the name" (Acts 5:41). The suffering of Christians soon went beyond dishonor to martyrdom with the stoning of Stephen. Paul, too, was called to a ministry of suffering. God instructed Ananias to care for Paul after his Damascus road experience. The risen Jesus said, "'I will show him how much he must suffer for the sake of my name'" (Acts 9:16). No wonder Paul could say that "we rejoice in our sufferings, knowing that suffering produces endurance, and endurance

Baptist Church Life and Leadership

produces character, and character produces hope, and hope does not disappoint us, because God's love has been poured into our hearts through the Holy Spirit which has been given to us" (Rom. 5:3–5). He saw suffering as an important part of discipleship; indeed, "we are children of God, and if children, then heirs, heirs of God and fellow heirs with Christ, provided we suffer with him in order that we may also be glorified with him" (Rom. 8:16–17).

Suffering is not merely an individual matter in communities of faith. When writing to the Corinthian church, Paul said, "If one member suffers, all suffer together" (1 Cor. 12:26). Later, in 2 Corinthians 1:6, he wrote, "If we are afflicted, it is for your comfort and salvation." Then he turned the conversation around: "Our hope for you is unshaken; for we know that as you share in our sufferings, you will also share in our comfort" (2 Cor. 1:7).

With suffering as its theme, 1 Peter seems to have been written to encourage Christians who were about to experience great persecution. The writer encouraged them by saying that "if when you do right and suffer for it you take it patiently, you have God's approval" (1 Pet. 2:20). Again, "But even if you do suffer for righteousness' sake, you will be blessed" (3:14).

The Epistle to the Hebrews also was written to persecuted Christians. One problem was whether Christians would disclaim the significance of the church and claim instead that Christianity was a Jewish sect. The writer made much of the sacrifice of Jesus as replacing the Jewish sacrifices. That sacrifice was made "once for all." Put clearly, "we have been sanctified through the offering of the body of Jesus Christ once for all" (10:10).

When God's people face criticism, hardship, pain, deprivation, political tyranny, the wounds of disrupted fellowship, or sorrow, they are not alone. In Galatians 6:2, Paul told Christians to "bear one another's burdens." Bearing burdens requires both compassion and action. When others hurt, all hurt. Caring for burdened persons is costly business. Whether in Albania, India, Liberia, Romania, South Africa, or China, such costly fellowship of suffering is still true in the life of the church. When some Christians suffer persecution, famine, injustice, poverty, or disease, it is the business of the entire church to respond and care for them.

The New Testament ideal is a free church in a free state. When Jesus said, "'Render therefore to Caesar the things that are Caesar's, and to God the things that are God's'" (Matt. 22:21), he knew that the Christian

73

life would be lived under tension. Most Christians since the time of Christ have lived without that ideal. Many have lived under the tyranny of a state or a state religion. Even now, countless Baptist Christians live where there is no free church in a free state. How grateful we should be for the Christians who have suffered grievous conditions and yet have shown their faithfulness.

True Christian leaders do not merely live off the sacrifices of others but willingly sacrifice themselves. Because there are lost people in the world, Christians on mission may pay dearly to witness. Because there are distressed Christians in the world, Christian leaders suffer. When they suffer, they sacrifice. The Bible is thus a challenge for Baptist Christians around the world. What does it mean to you?

BUILDING ON THE FOUNDATIONS

We have examined five pillars of faith which are foundational in church life and leadership. Doing what a church is supposed to do involves: reaching people for the Savior, baptizing them, and discipling them into church membership; sending them into the community as God's servant-ambassadors; empowering them by God's Spirit; ministering together; and risking costly discipleship. An effective church is linked to biblical Christianity. Still, we must face reality: leaders dedicated to these enduring ideals often work in less than ideal conditions.

Paul the apostle was a church planter and early pastor extraordinary. He enjoyed being with people whom he had won to faith, like Christians in Corinth, but, on occasion, explained a delay in his travels. "But I will stay in Ephesus . . . , for a wide door for effective work has opened to me, and there are many adversaries" (1 Cor. 16:8–9). Adversity may come today in the guise of accident or illness, political tyranny, personal danger, loss of property, position, or possessions, betrayal by fellow church members, and even outright opposition to one's leadership style or vision from God.

Churches entering the twenty-first century face great diversity of cultural contexts, past history, leadership styles, levels of members' spirituality, financial resources, and congregational hopes and unrealized dreams. Yet, the lure of God's kingdom ideal retains its luster. In the most trying circumstances, people want and need to experience God. When faith's lamp flickers in one land, encouraging news of marvelous Christian victories reaches us from China, Kenya, South

Baptist Church Life and Leadership

Korea, Liberia, Brazil, and elsewhere. We are encouraged to remain faithful to the finish, so that we do not lose heart.

The church's task is to reach persons and families in many lands with the gospel. But it is more than that. It must touch cultures and transform societies with enduring Christian values. It is even more than that. Church leaders of the future face an increasingly complex, mobile world population that expects more options and offers more challenges, generation by generation. Yet, God's challenge to us is as fresh as tomorrow's hope, "'Behold . . . you may be tested, . . . and will have tribulation. Be faithful unto death, and I will give you the crown of life'" (Rev. 2:10).

CHAPTER SIX

Human Rights for All

EVERY DAY THE NEWS MEDIA CONFRONT US WITH TERRIBLE hurts that are inflicted on brothers and sisters of the human family. We know that all intricacies of modern technology are used to devise ever more effective instruments of torture to maim and break the bodies and spirits of men, women, and children. We know that ideologies of racism, apartheid, and sexism deny equal chances to millions of people. We know that day by day, students, workers, pastors, and journalists disappear and are never seen again. We know of millions of refugees and asylum seekers who exist under inhuman conditions and who, in addition, are despised as the outcasts of modern human society. We know of the increasing rate of unemployment, casting millions of people into a crisis of identity, and robbing them of a chance to care for themselves and for their families.

In addition, we know that in all corners of our globe people are denied the religious liberty to worship and live the way their religious impulses demand. We know that the arms race by its costly diversion of funds is in effect taking human lives. While the governments of the world spend billions of dollars to create ever more sophisticated and destructive weapons, two-thirds of humankind are sinking deeper into poverty and disillusionment. We know that twelve million children under the age of five die each year—almost thirty-five thousand each day—because they do not have enough food, sufficient clean water, and adequate medical care; and many of those who survive are exploited through child labor and child prostitution.

Human Rights for All

WE ARE RESPONSIBLE FOR WHAT WE KNOW

Yet we as Christians also have another kind of knowledge, the knowledge of faith in Christ. We confess that God has created the world. In beautiful language the creation story tells us that "God saw everything that he had made, and behold, it was very good" (Gen. 1:31, RSV). This goodness is God's gift to us. We must protect it, and where it is damaged, we must restore it. It is a cause for great concern that we as humans have been very selfish. With pride and arrogance, we have arrogated divinity to ourselves; we have hated, tortured, and killed each other; and we have been disrespectful of the garden of nature in which God has placed us. We have even killed Jesus, the man who had no other passion than to love God and his fellow human beings. Yet God has not given up on his creation. By raising Jesus from the dead, God has confirmed his purposes for the world. In Christ, God has reconciled the world with himself (2 Cor. 5:17–21).

It is our responsibility to relate our knowledge of the world and our knowledge of God to each other. Sadly, few Christians have committed themselves to the modern struggle for human rights. They have not yet related their knowledge of God to their knowledge of what is happening in God's world. The knowledge of faith includes the conviction that the "earth is the Lord's and the fullness thereof, the world and those who dwell therein" (Ps. 24:1), but somehow many of us have failed to interrelate our faith in God with the struggle for human rights in the world.

That, however, is a luxury which we can no longer afford. The responsibility of knowledge is an inherent aspect of faith. "Whoever knows what is right to do and fails to do it, for him it is sin" (James 4:17). Today's challenge is: can the human race survive in a humane manner, or will the spiral of selfishness, violence, and mistrust accelerate beyond our control? The will to live is instilled in all of us. Often we deform it to serve our own selfish interests. We, therefore, need a vision of human life on earth that transcends our immediate national, social, and religious interests and that helps us to develop structures that make human life possible for all people.

THE BAPTIST VISION AND HUMAN RIGHTS

The struggle for human rights has been part of shaping the Baptist vision. The origins of the Baptist vision on the European continent, in the British isles, and in North America are closely linked to the claim of religious

WE BAPTISTS

liberty. The Anabaptists in sixteenth-century continental Europe and the Baptists in seventeenth-century England followed Christ as the one and only voice of their consciences even when this led to conflicts with the monarchy, the governments, and the established churches. Thomas Helwys's (1550?–1616) *A Short Declaration of the Mistery of Iniquity* (1612) has been hailed as the first Protestant defense of religious liberty. The struggle for religious liberty was taken to the North American colonies, and there, through the work of people like Roger Williams (1603?–1683), it became an important element shaping the Baptist vision.

When we as Baptists become convinced that our consciences, bound to and informed by the word of God, lead us in a certain direction, then we will try to set out on that pilgrimage, even when this brings us into conflict with the institutions of society, state, and church. This struggle for religious liberty has become an important element in shaping modern human rights as human beings attempt to define and protect human dignity against the onslaught of dehumanizing institutions.

HUMAN RIGHTS SPELLED OUT

Human rights are spelled out in the various human rights instruments. Resulting from the massive disrespect for human rights in World War II, the United Nations (1945) was founded with the declared purpose:

WE THE PEOPLES OF THE UNITED NATIONS DETERMINED

to save succeeding generations from the scourge of war, which twice in our lifetime has brought untold sorrow to mankind, and

to reaffirm faith in fundamental human rights, in the dignity and worth of the human person, in the equal rights of men and women and of nations large and small, and

to establish conditions under which justice and respect for the obligations arising from treaties and other sources of international law can be maintained, and to promote social progress and better standards of life in larger freedom,

AND FOR THESE ENDS

to practice tolerance and live together in peace with one another as good neighbors, and

Human Rights for All

to unite our strength to maintain international peace and security, and to ensure, by the acceptance of the principles and the institution of methods, that armed force shall not be used, save in the common interest, and

to employ international machinery for the promotion of the economic and social advancement of all peoples,

HAVE RESOLVED TO COMBINE OUR EFFORTS TO ACCOMPLISH THESE AIMS. (Preamble to the Charter of the United Nations, 1945)

In 1948, the *Universal Declaration of Human Rights* was proclaimed. In 1998, we celebrated the fiftieth anniversary of this declaration, which has been hailed as "one of the most important instruments and landmarks in the history of mankind."[1] It sets a standard of morality by which nations should measure their treatment of citizens and by which citizens can know their own rights over against the state and the human community.

This declaration was followed eighteen years later, in 1966, by two covenants, the *International Covenant of Economic, Social, and Cultural Rights* and the *International Covenant on Civil and Political Rights*, together with the *Optional Protocol* to the latter covenant. For governments that have ratified it, this protocol allows individual persons to file complaints in human rights matters with an international Human Rights Committee. Together with the *Universal Declaration*, these covenants form the *International Bill of Human Rights*, which sets a moral and juridical standard for the human community. More than one hundred nations have ratified these covenants and have thereby promised to use all available urgency to implement these human rights in their areas of jurisdiction.

The *Universal Declaration* and the covenants are backed up by many more declarations and conventions that deal with the definition and effective implementation of individual human rights. Recent examples are the *Declaration on the Elimination of All Forms of Intolerance and Discrimination Based on Religion or Belief* (1981), the *Convention against Torture and Other Cruel, Inhuman or Degrading Treatment or Punishment* (1984), and the *Convention on the Rights of the Child* (1989). Conventions on religious liberty and on conscientious objection are in the process of preparation.

---

1. Seán MacBride, "The Universal Declaration—30 Years After," in Alan D. Falconer, ed., *Understanding Human Rights: An Interdisciplinary and Interfaith Study* (Dublin: Irish School of Ecumenics, 1980), p. 10.

WE BAPTISTS

THE CONTENT OF HUMAN RIGHTS

What then is the content of human rights? For convenience, we may distinguish between individual rights, social rights, rights that show a special regard for the developing countries, the rights of nature, and rights of future generations.

Individual rights are designed to protect the dignity of the individual over against human and historical institutions like state and church, party and crown. They include the right to life, the right to freedom of thought, opinion, conscience, and religion, the right of people to participate freely in free and frequent elections, the right to privacy and to fairness before the law, the right to equality, and the prohibition of torture, slavery, and arbitrary arrests.

Then there are the social rights. These include the right to work and to fair pay, the right to leisure, the right to form trade unions, and the rights to social security, education, proper medical treatment, and free participation in the life of the community.

Besides the individual and the social rights, there are rights that show special concern for the developing nations in the Two-thirds World. These nations feel themselves caught in a never-ending spiral of dependence. For decades, they were caught in the cold war between the superpowers, and they suffer under an unjust world economic order. For many in the Two-thirds World, the individual and social rights appear to be unobtainable luxuries. What good is the right to free speech if you cannot read or write and have no way to receive information? What good is the right to life if you have no food, no water, and no medical facilities? What good is the right to a national identity if you belong to the twelve million refugees who are considered the outcasts of modern human society? Human rights, therefore, also include rights such as the right to self-determination of nations, the right to a national identity, the right to asylum, and the rights to the basic necessities like food, water, shelter, and medical treatment to make a life of human dignity possible.

During recent years, the human community has begun to understand that God has placed us in a garden (that is, nature), and, if we exploit and destroy this garden, we are presumptuous in our disrespect for God's creation, and, at the same time, we are destroying ourselves. The air we breathe, the water we drink, the vegetables we eat, all become part of ourselves. We are intimately woven into the fabric of nature. But with our focus on ourselves, on history, and on progress, we have

Human Rights for All

exploited nature so much that the term "ecology crisis" is an understatement. The United Nations with the special impetus from ecology summits held in Rio de Janeiro (1993) and Kyoto (1997) is in the process of developing rights of nature.

Let us not forget. Whatever we do or leave undone, we so determine the life of future generations, our children and grandchildren. The tremendous debts which most developing countries have can never be paid back. They strangle the children before they are born. Nuclear technology creates wastes with deadly radiation that lasts for thousands of years. The cutting of the rain forests, the desertification, and the thinning of the ozone layer create climatic conditions which may spell doom for our children and grandchildren. Hence, we must in all our decisions now consider the rights of future generations.

WHY WE NEED HUMAN RIGHTS

But do we need human rights to protect human beings whose lives and dignity are threatened and whose future is bleak? Is it not enough to preach the gospel and then expect God to take care of what he wants to have done? Such an attitude would be both unbiblical and unrealistic.

This attitude is unbiblical because the Christian story as it comes to us through the Scriptures tells us in ever new variations that God's word has become flesh in a special way in Jesus Christ and aims to become flesh ever again through those who follow Christ. God's will aims to become concrete. God, therefore, elects people to do his will on earth. Jesus both talked about God's forgiveness and healing and concretely forgave and healed. In his healing and saving work in the world, God does not bypass us, but he calls us to join his passion for the world and become "fellow workers" with him (1 Cor. 3:9).

This attitude is also unrealistic to limit the church's ministry to the preaching of the word. Our faith in Jesus Christ has made us sensitive to the power of human selfishness and our human unwillingness to help others. Our self-interest colors everything we do. Our world seems to have become a place in which only the fit can survive and only the strong can be free. Our gods, that is, those strongholds that we trust and to which we entrust our future, are militarism, consumerism, money, and power. In such a world, we are called to live out our commitment to the First Commandment and to assert in word and in deed that as far as we are concerned Jesus Christ is the way, the truth, and the life (Exod. 20:2–3;

WE BAPTISTS

John 14:6). The only way to protect those who have no power, no voice, and no friends is to create structures that can bridle and reshape the present structures of injustice.

We may presume that human rights are part of God's providential working in history to make and to keep human life human. Since God does not bypass us in his working in the world, we are all invited to join in his work by engaging ourselves in the implementation of human rights. The prophets summarize the divine imperative for us: "what does the Lord require of you but to do justice, and to love kindness, and to walk humbly with your God?" (Mic. 6:8); "but let justice roll down like waters, and righteousness like an everflowing stream" (Amos 5:2).

WHY CHRISTIANS SHOULD BE CONCERNED ABOUT HUMAN RIGHTS

We have seen that human rights have become a welcome reality in our world. Many hopes are focused on their implementation. Can they help to bridle the selfishness of individuals and nations and point a way forward to a better future? What attitude should we as Christians adopt toward the struggle for human rights? Is the struggle for the codification, the protection, and the implementation of human rights an essential part of our faith in Jesus Christ? As Baptists, we look into the biblical message to find answers to such questions.

In Scripture we find that God has a passion to make human life human. When God's people are oppressed, God longs for their liberation, and he invites people like Moses to participate in that liberating activity. With the law codes in Israel, special care is taken to ease the fate of the poor, the slave, the orphan, the widow, and the stranger. The prophets condemn those leaders in religious, economic, and political institutions who are not concerned with protecting the dignity of human persons.

Jesus announces liberation to the oppressed (Luke 4:18–19) and promises grace to the poor, to the hungry, and to the sorrowful (Luke 6:20–21). He fleshes out the gospel by healing the sick, driving out demons, and sharing his life with the marginal people of society.

The earliest Christian churches tuned into Jesus' passion for the world by affirming the essential equality of all persons and by beginning to eliminate injustice from their own midst. When the resurrection of the crucified Christ became historically manifest, Christian communities

Human Rights for All

emerged in which racial, social, or sexual barriers and injustices were transfigured into a new reality of life together because in Christ there "is neither Jew nor Greek, there is neither slave nor free, there is neither male nor female" (Gal. 3:28).

Indeed, we may safely say that the psalmist gathers up the tendency and the intention of the whole biblical message when he hears God speaking to his conscience: "Give justice to the weak and the fatherless; maintain the right of the afflicted and the destitute" (Ps. 82:3). The writer of Proverbs relates this directly to God's action in history: "the Lord will plead their cause" (22:23). Moreover, "he who oppresses a poor man insults his Maker, but he who is kind to the needy honors him" (Prov. 14:31). Thus, tuning into God's healing and saving passion for the world is the privilege of faith. By our attitude and action, we reveal who our God is.

The earliest Christian churches consciously located Jesus' presence in the world both in the preaching of the word and the administration of the ordinances and in the child (Mark 9:36–37), the hungry, the stranger, the naked, and the prisoner. Inasmuch as we have done it or not done it to these, his brothers and sisters through the ages, we have done it or not done it to him (Matt. 25:31–46). If the church wants to be found where Jesus Christ is active in the world, then it must show healing, saving, and liberating solidarity with those whose human dignity is injured or threatened.

WHAT BAPTISTS ARE DOING ABOUT HUMAN RIGHTS

Along many other Christian churches and nongovernmental organizations, Baptists are involved in the struggle for human rights. Many of our people are affected by the denial of human rights. Christians in countries where other religions dominate are denied religious liberty; the same may be true where one Christian church denies equality to members of other Christian churches. Some of our brothers and sisters live in refugee camps; they have no identity, have no passport, and live under the constant threat of being shot or burned. Many Baptists are living in areas of racial and ethnic conflict and suffer in the explosion of racial and ethnic hatred.

There is a growing awareness in our midst that if one suffers, all suffer, and if one is honored, all rejoice (1 Cor. 12:26). In many of our churches, we find men, women, and young people who are concretely engaged in

WE BAPTISTS

the struggle to attain religious liberty, to protect children, to help refugees and asylum seekers, and to resist apartheid, racism, sexism, and torture.

The Baptist World Alliance (BWA) has recognized this concern in our tradition and in our churches by creating a Human Rights Commission. This commission, made up of about one hundred Baptist leaders, meets once a year to discuss issues, hear reports, prepare statements or resolutions, and decide on appropriate actions.

During recent years, for instance, the Human Rights Commission has discussed historical matters such as the contribution that Baptists have made to the human rights tradition. It has dealt with different theological approaches to human rights. It has informed itself about Baptist contributions to the work of the United Nations. It has dealt with issues like torture, shelter for the homeless, equality of men and women in our churches, the problems of children in our world, and the fate of refugees and asylum seekers. It has heard and discussed reports given by Baptist leaders from Bulgaria, Myanmar (Burma), Thailand, Bangladesh, Nagaland, Rwanda, Burundi, Liberia, Philippines, Nicaragua, El Salvador, Cuba, Jordan, South Africa, and the Caribbean. It has investigated what better procedures could be found to inform our unions/conventions and our churches about the need to become involved in the struggle for human rights.

The BWA recommends to all Baptist churches that every year in December (the Universal Declaration on Human Rights was adopted on December 10, 1948), a Human Rights Sunday be observed. A special worship service with a human rights emphasis can be conducted. The Human Rights Commission prepares suggestions for liturgy and sermon, which are sent out to all Baptist unions/conventions and Baptist editors, who, in turn, are encouraged to make this information available to the churches.

Every year an official BWA human rights visit is made to an area in which our people and our churches live in difficult situations. BWA leaders visit churches to encourage them and bring to them our international Baptist solidarity. They visit government officials to plead for those whose human rights are denied, and they disseminate to our member churches what they have seen and heard. Recently, such visits have been made to Cuba, to the refugee camps at the Thai-Burmese border, and to Mexico, Bulgaria, Lebanon, El Salvador, Myanmar (Burma), Macedonia, and Syria.

Every five years at the Baptist world congress, a Human Rights Award is given to a person from our midst "for significant and effective

Human Rights for All

activities to secure, protect, restore, or preserve human rights." This is a significant honor.

The Human Rights Commission carefully listens to the stories of our brothers and sisters who are hurting, and it tries to find ways to alleviate the pain and lighten the burden. The commission also produces literature which informs our churches about human rights and what they can do to implement them.

Above all, through our traditional emphasis on evangelism, missions, and community, we make a constructive contribution to the human rights movement. We preach the gospel because we believe that a living faith in God is an essential part of human dignity. We engage in holistic mission because salvation means the healing of the whole person. We try to reflect the love of God for all people by being open communities in which people can discover meaning, hope, and liberation. We believe that the closer we come to Christ the more passionate we become in our concern for making whole the lives of people.

THE REMAINING TASK

Despite many efforts by many people, the greatest problem related to human rights is the universal reluctance and failure to implement them. Even those nations that have ratified the covenants and other human rights instruments sometimes blatantly disregard their commitments and fail to be true to their promises. The United Nations has little power to enforce human rights, because the structures of implementation are still inadequate. Nevertheless, we cannot afford the luxury of resignation. Especially we who believe that God, the creator of heaven and earth, has not abandoned his creation should be motivated by hope, faith, and love to create analogies to the kingdom of God in our world, to foreshadow his saving passion, and thus to prepare the way of the Lord. What can we as Christians and as churches do for the implementation of human rights? We can become aware through teaching and information. We can form groups that pray and work for specific projects or for specific people whose human rights are being denied. We can creatively participate in shaping a new theology that makes God's concern for the marginalized an essential part of our thinking about Christian faith. We must find ways to bring our performance into harmony with our message and thus enhance the credibility of the church. We also can add to the prophetic function of the church by reminding our governments of their responsibilities and by uncovering and publicizing human rights violations.

Let us also gratefully join others who are effectively engaged in the struggle for human rights. Having discerned God's providential activity in and through the human rights tradition, having heard God's invitation to join the struggle to heal human life, and having been obedient to his call, we then gratefully find many others who are engaged in the same struggle. We can help them and learn from their expertise. With Amnesty International, the International Commission of Jurists, and Christians for the Abolition of Torture, we can work to eradicate torture and help those whose religious liberty is being denied. Along with the many children's organizations, we can help to implement the rights of the child. We can support the United Nations and the World Council of Churches in their efforts to help refugees and to eradicate racism. We can support Green Peace in the necessary effort to protect the environment. If we make this concern for human rights part of our Christian agenda, we will soon discover ways to become involved.

CONCLUSION

As Baptists we are committed to the biblical message as God's word to us. This is a word that forgives our sin and liberates us from our self-interest so that we can creatively tune into God's healing passion for the world. At the same time, we are a worldwide fellowship of believers in which we feel the agony and the joys of our brothers and sisters around the world: "If one member suffers, all suffer together; if one member is honored, all rejoice together" (1 Cor. 12:26). The closer we come to Christ, the more we shall hear the silent and spoken cries of men, women, and children for whom Christ died. In our faith, our prayer, and our life, we can no longer bypass those whose human dignity is being denied. Our commitment to the struggle for the implementation of human rights becomes an essential part of our faith in the trinitarian God.

Suggestions for Further Reading

Baptist Heritage

Estep, William R., Jr. *The Anabaptist Story: An Introduction to Sixteenth-Century Anabaptism.* 3d ed. Grand Rapids, MI: William B. Eerdmans Publishing Company, 1996.

McBeth, H. Leon. *The Baptist Heritage: Four Centuries of Baptist Witness.* Nashville, TN: Broadman Press, 1987.

Wardin, Albert W., ed. *Baptists around the World: A Comprehensive Handbook.* Nashville, TN: Broadman and Holman Publishers, 1995.

Baptist Doctrine

Beasley-Murray, Paul. *Radical Believers: The Baptist Way of Being the Church.* Didcot, U. K.: Baptist Union of Great Britain, 1992.

Bush, L. Russ, III, and Tom J. Nettles. *Baptists and the Bible.* Rev. ed. Nashville, TN: Broadman and Holman Publishers, 1999.

Deweese, Charles W., ed. *Defining Baptist Convictions: Guidelines for the Twenty-First Century.* Franklin, TN: Providence House Publishers, 1996.

Lumpkin, William L. *Baptist Confessions of Faith.* Rev. ed. Valley Forge, PA: Judson Press, 1983.

Tuck, William Powell. *Our Baptist Tradition.* Macon, GA: Smyth and Helwys Publishing, Inc., 1993.

Christian Ethics

Brown, Colin. *Living in Love and Justice.* Didcot, U. K.: Baptist Union of Great Britain, 1998.

Geisler, Norman L. *Christian Ethics: Options and Issues.* Grand Rapids, MI: Baker Book House, 1989.

WE BAPTISTS

Grenz, Stanley. *The Moral Quest: Foundations of Christian Ethics.* Downers Grove, IL: InterVarsity Press, 1997.

Higgins, Ray. *Turn Right: A Christian Guide for Making Better Decisions.* Nashville, TN: Baptist Center for Ethics, 1994.

Baptist Worship

Basden, Paul A. "'Something Old, Something New': Worship Styles for Baptists in the Nineties." In *Ties That Bind: Life Together in the Baptist Vision,* ed. by Gary A. Furr and Curtis W. Freeman. Macon, GA: Smyth and Helwys Publishing, Inc., 1994.

Cupit, L. A. (Tony), ed. *Hallowed Be Your Name: A Collection of Prayers from around the World.* McLean, VA: Baptist World Alliance, 1998.

Furr, Gary A. and Milburn Price. *The Dialogue of Worship: Creating Space for Revelation and Response.* Macon, GA: Smyth and Helwys Publishing, Inc., 1998.

Martin, Ralph P. *Worship in the Early Church.* Rev. ed. Grand Rapids, MI: William B. Eerdmans Publishing Co., 1975.

Segler, Franklin M. *Understanding, Preparing for, and Practicing Christian Worship.* Rev. by Randall Bradley. Nashville, TN: Broadman and Holman Publishers, 1996.

Church Life and Leadership

Augsburger, David. *Conflict Mediation across Cultures.* Louisville, KY: Westminster/John Knox Press, 1992.

Dale, Robert D. *Leadership for a Changing Church: Charting the Shape of the River.* Nashville, TN: Abingdon Press, 1998.

Giles, Kevin. *Patterns of Ministry among the First Christians.* Melbourne, Australia: Collins Dove, 1989.

McNeal, Reggie. *Revolution in Leadership: Creating Apostles for Tomorrow's Churches.* Nashville, TN: Abingdon Press, 1998.

Human Rights

Human Rights: A Compilation of International Instruments. New York, NY: United Nations, 1978.

The International Bill of Human Rights. New York, NY: United Nations, 1978.

Life in All Its Fullness: The Word of God and Human Rights. New York, NY: American Bible Society, 1992.

Tiller, Carl W. *The Bible and the Universal Declaration of Human Rights.* McLean, VA: Baptist World Alliance, 1995.

Wood, James E., Jr. *Baptists and Human Rights.* McLean, VA: Baptist World Alliance, 1997.